THE

RESOLUTION FOR WOMEN

New Revised Edition

PRISCILLA SHIRER

PUBLISHING
BRENTWOOD, TENNESSEE

For Lois & Mary

❧ ACKNOWLEDGMENTS ❧

Jerry. Thank you for loving and supporting me as I've fumbled my way through marriage, motherhood, and ministry. You have been a brick wall of support and refuge as I've sought to honor God and you and to walk beside you in life and love. I'm forever grateful for you. Thank you for encouraging me to be a woman of resolution.

Jackson, Jerry Jr., Jude. When I first wrote this book, you were all under ten years old. Now a decade later, the three of you have blossomed into young manhood in the most spectacular way. My life's seminal aspiration has been to serve you well. And while I haven't been perfect at it, I pray that I've been consistent. My hope is that the resolutions your father and I have made concerning you and our family will have ripple effects that will bless your children and your children's children. We are both nuts about you and are thrilled to behold the men of resolution that you are becoming.

Alex and Stephen Kendrick. I am still stunned that God has allowed my ministry to intersect with yours, on paper and on screen. I am completely aware that the breadth of ministry the Lord has entrusted to me is largely because of your vision and leadership. You have increased our territory and broadened our reach. Jerry and I are both grateful and honored to partner with you.

Lawrence. Every publishing project is a journey, and walking alongside you in this decade-old one has been a gift that keeps on giving. Thank you for living a life of resolution as a writer, husband, father, and follower of Jesus. Your patience, humility, spiritual sensitivity, and excellence inspire me in more ways than you can imagine.

And my sister-friends—some younger, others older, some single and others married, some moms and others not—who met with me ten years ago over dinner to offer your sentiments, personal experiences, and insights for this project, I say thank you. Hundreds of thousands of women have been challenged by the resolutions that were birthed out of our conversation. And now there will be a fresh crop of ladies who will digest them for the first (or second) time and recalibrate their lives because of them. In the last decade, we've raised children, cultivated our marriages, lost loved ones, battled difficult diagnoses, struggled through disappointment, and celebrated each other's joys. You have been women of resolution, and your faithfulness continues to inspire me every day. Thank you for lending your perspectives and opening up your lives to me. The richness of your lives is the crowning treasure of this book.

Finally, B&H Publishing Team. Thank you for publishing this book . . . again. There are a host of women who were too young to notice it the first time around. Who knows if they might grab hold of it this time around, both in their hands and their hearts. Jerry and I treasure you and are grateful to partner with you.

CONTENTS

PART II: *This is what I have.*

PART III: *This is what matters to me.*

❧ FOREWORD ❧

One name kept coming up in our conversations.

It was ten years ago. We were deep into the making of the feature film *Courageous* while simultaneously crafting a companion book to help men step up and become stronger fathers and husbands. But we needed help. *The Resolution for Men* was only part of the battle. How could we also support and encourage women in their many vital roles in the family?

We were writing to men. We needed a strong, godly, female voice, someone who was grounded in the Word and could speak directly to women. As we prayed and sought counsel, the same name kept rising to the top as the perfect writer for *The Resolution for Women*.

Priscilla Shirer.

We didn't realize at the time the wonderful blessing she would become to us.

It was through her partnership on this landmark book that our friendship with Priscilla and her husband, Jerry, began. And by God's grace, He not only used this book to bless countless women but sparked our joyful ministry partnership. Priscilla later stepped into our movie ministry and gave us wonderful performances in *War Room* and *Overcomer* that touched lives around the world. She also partnered with us on her powerful books *Fervent* and *Radiant*. Truly the Lord has enhanced our lives through Priscilla's ministry gifts, encouragement, and tremendous love for the Lord.

This ten-year revision of a true classic is the latest. And we are grateful for what He is going to do through this updated edition to bless women like you.

We invite you to warm up a fresh cup of coffee. Find a quiet place to focus. Then open your heart and ask God to do a fresh, renewed work in you as you read. May you be blessed, encouraged, and challenged by Priscilla's words and by the God she so deeply loves and serves!

Alex Kendrick
Stephen Kendrick

A NOTE *from* PRISCILLA

If I could go back and give my mid-twenty-year-old self a helpful word or two of advice, here's what I'd tell her. . . .

Don't forget to stretch.

I've always been an active person. Back in my school days, I participated in a handful of competitive sports and extracurricular activities: track and field, gymnastics, cheerleading, basketball, and volleyball. As every athletic season dovetailed into the next, I'd immerse myself into whichever activity was currently on the front burner, engaging the unique physical demands of each one.

One common thread, however, ran throughout all of them—at every practice, every game, every warm-up for every competition. Every time.

Stretching.

We always had to stretch.

Depending on the sport, our coaches would guide us through stretching routines and drills specific to that discipline, sometimes specific to that day's emphasis. Several of the techniques were similar across the board—general stretches for our arms, legs, and core—but many of them focused precisely on the muscle groups that were most involved in performing our roles in that particular sport. We were told that a commitment to stretching would help us maintain flexibility, enhance agility, and cultivate a full range of motion, not to mention stave off injury. For all these reasons and more, we never skipped the stretching portion of our workout, no matter the sport. Ever.

But then I grew up and became a twentyish woman who was busy with the details of a burgeoning life. I wasn't playing sports any longer, but I still exercised fairly regularly, hoping to burn calories and manage my weight.

By the time I was nearing thirty, my husband and I had begun growing a family. One kid became three in fairly quick succession. Given this new dynamic, I felt that I had to take advantage of any spare moment I could convert into exercise, jumping into a cardio routine that accelerated my metabolism, burned calories, and kept my favorite jeans fitting just right. I'd burst out of my front door before dawn and jog around the neighborhood. Then when I got back, I'd drop to the grass for a few quick rounds of push-ups and sit-ups before heading inside. My shirt would always be soaked with sweat, my thighs alight with the buzz of feel-good adrenaline and endorphins. My blood was pumping and I was ready to launch into the day. Ahead of the game, right out of the gate. Mission accomplished.

Except I hadn't stretched. Didn't see the need. Wasn't a priority.

Because who had the time? Not me, that's who.

During the next decade of my life, as God gave new ministry opportunities, my family and I were often out traveling with our three sons in tow. A few days each month, hotel workout rooms and vast convention center parking lots replaced my neighborhood streets and yard as available exercise venues. Thirty minutes here, forty-five minutes there, I'd periodically break away for a heart-pounding workout routine, rushing into my usual intervals and exercises without any meaningful attempt at stretching myself out first.

Then came the forties. And this new decade brought a new set of physical challenges. For one, my knees turned tender and inflamed. I quickly realized I'd better lay off the jogging and revamp my program to something less traumatic on my joints and more conducive to my long-term health and fitness goals. The only problem was that I'd been doing the same kinds of exercises for so long that I was bit lost on how to shift to a new regimen. I needed help breaking out of the rut.

So I enlisted a trainer, Troy, to help me shake up my routine. And on our very first session, on our very first day, in our very first minutes together, what do you think Troy did? He stretched me. Pushed my limbs far beyond their comfortable range, forcing my muscles to lengthen and elongate. Twice each week, over the next four years, he spent the first fifteen minutes of every workout advising and assisting me with movements designed to increase flexibility in my hamstrings, glutes, quads, calves, and shoulders.

And I'll be honest, after those fifteen solid minutes of introductory work, I always wanted to quit. If I'd had it my way, I would've packed up my bag, walked right out the door, and dragged my limp extremities to the nearest Krispy Kreme. After twenty years of neglecting stretching, each repetition felt like fire screaming through my body. The discomfort was palatable. Painful. Every time.

Stretching *became* the workout. At least it sure did feel like one.

Truth is, stretching feels that way, in all areas of life. Any time we push past our comfort point—personally, creatively, spiritually, relationally, emotionally, mentally, and, yes, physically—we're apt to feel a resistance that causes us to favor complacency. Stretching requires intentionality and willingness to experience an uneasiness that few people are interested in pursuing. Because, let's be honest, *not* stretching is easier. But if we don't commit to this discipline of stretching ourselves, even as far back as our twenties and thirties, a certain rigidity will naturally slip in as we move into our forties, fifties, sixties, and beyond. Just like my various coaches warned me throughout high school, we'll look up one day and realize . . .

- We've lost our *flexibility*. We won't be as able to adjust gracefully and with ease during the many shifts and changes that each season of our lives will call for. Our hearts will seize up, hardening with resentment toward those around us. We'll feel ourselves being pulled out of our routines and established patterns, out of the habits we're most comfortable and settled in, and we'll reflexively resist. Even if we know we should adapt our expectations, the built-in rigidity becomes a huge obstacle to overcome. It will draw us back, make us feel stuck and held down, even if a change of course is what's truly best for us, perhaps even required of us.

- We've lost our *agility*. Our quickness to respond. Sometimes the challenge in front of us won't wait. We need to move;

we need to act. But if we haven't been keeping our joints lubricated, we're liable to be caught off guard, unable and unwilling to respond to the need of the moment. Only through ordinary and incremental stretching, on days when we're not under the gun, do we build up the reserve of conviction and wisdom that can spring into the nimble action that life often requires. Stretching keeps us sensitive and anticipating. Primed, principled, decisive.

• We've lost our *range of motion*. Life is complicated. As soon as we focus on any one thing and start feeling pretty good about it, ten other aspects of our lives have sprung a leak and started to deteriorate. It's tough. What we need, and what God frees us to do if we'll cooperate with Him, is to increase our capacity, to take a whole-life approach that keeps everything moving in a faithful direction, all the way around, so that growth in any one area bleeds naturally into all the others.

• We are prone to *injury*. Instead of people's hurtful comments rolling off our backs, dropping powerless to the ground, we'll bristle at every real or imagined slight. Instead of having a capacity for feeling others' needs and injustices, we'll be too sidelined with our own aches and pains to care. But like with my strained and pained knees, the discipline of stretching decreases our inflammation, takes some of the pressure off, and eases some of the tenderness that makes us so easy to wound. It limbers us up and keeps us from feeling unnecessary aggravation.

If we'll *only. keep. stretching.*

Because here's the deal: our physical muscles naturally stagnate with age. It just happens. The tightness, the stiffness. Time does it without our help, simply while we're out there living. We don't need to do anything to facilitate it—*EXCEPT not stretch*. The same is true about life. Without intentionally, consistently reaching and stretching toward God's best for us and those around us, we'll harden over time.

But that's why I'm here. And hopefully why you're here too.

No matter your age or stage of life, this book is an invitation to s-t-r-e-t-c-h, to extend yourself in those places where you've been either too busy or too distracted to think deeply, to press onward and upward, to sharpen your gifts and talents, to pursue God's best for yourself and those you love. I want you *stretching* in ways that will yield God-honoring outcomes both now and throughout your lifetimes.

Looking back, I'm so grateful for the way that some of my wisest mentors kept challenging me to reach higher in different areas of my life. I'm even more grateful for how the Lord, in His sovereign kindness and care, has continued to place me in scenarios and circumstances that have stretched me, challenged me, and matured me.

So as you turn each page of this book, consider me your trainer, enlisted to push you, to challenge you, to reach and press and pull you toward maturity so that you'll stay agile and unrestricted, growing healthily through your current season of life and into the ones yet to come.

That's what *The Resolution for Women* is all about.

And just like any good trainer, I want you to know what you're getting into, just in case you'd rather opt out before your first session begins. This book isn't for pleasure reading. In fact, some of it may not be very pleasurable at all. Sometimes it hurts to stretch, especially when someone else is pushing you in ways that feel uncomfortable. You'll most likely find it a bit antagonistic and convicting in spots.

I certainly have.

But I'm praying right here at the forefront that you'll make the choice to continue on with me, because I'm convinced that stretching ourselves with God-honoring resolves is worth it.

Even if you're not the resolution-making type.

Even if you're in relationship with someone who doesn't respect what you're doing and has no intention of making any resolutions of their own.

Even if you're a tad unconvinced that any of this will make one bit of difference.

Even if you're not in the mood for it and don't have the track record to back it up.

Even if you haven't stretched yourself like this in years.

Come with me anyway, on a resolution revolution journey that will be worth every step we take together. Why?

First, this resolution is with God. Unlike many of the New Year's variety, these resolutions are founded squarely on principles that God Himself has established. These are more than just determinations you make within yourself; they are girded about with the power of the Holy Spirit—encouraging you, comforting you, equipping you, empowering you with the strength you need to carry them out. Essentially, these are His resolutions for you.

Second, these resolutions will impact the people you love. If you're married, I'm talking about your husband. If you're a mom, I'm talking about your children. If you're single, I'm talking about your friends and family. Even if none of these people appear to actively admire or support your efforts in making these resolutions, you're going to be doing business with God and making decisions based on His Word. And the deep impact this will have on your life will overflow into the experiences of those around you. Sometimes the greatest miracle of all is the one that happens in your own heart, the change that takes place in you and then surprises you as it filters into the seams and fabric of your whole life. But the effects of a changed person on her surroundings can be staggering. The deep impact this resolution will have on your life will overflow into the experiences of those around you.

You may find yourself tempted as you read along to point a finger of blame and frustration in other people's direction. "What about my husband? Why isn't *he* inclined to change? Why is it always about what *I'm* supposed to be doing, instead of my family, my children, my coworkers, my friends? Aren't they a part of this equation too?" You may feel like rolling your eyes at the seemingly one-sided skew of some of the conversations we're going to have.

So let me just be clear. This book *is* slanted. It's decidedly and purposefully designed not to take into consideration the actions (or inactions) of the other members of your family or the people who live and work and go to church with you. I'm not going to be addressing your husband or how he should behave. This is about what *you* will do, who you will become by God's grace from this day forward. This is the *Resolution for WOMEN*. More specifically, one woman.

You.

And all you need to know and care about is that in God's impeccable timing and design, He has brought this book into your life for this particular season. He is going to stretch you in the themes that these chapters present, and you'll need a strong dose of courage to dare living them instead of throwing in the towel prematurely, packing up your gym bag, and (like me) wanting to head straight to the nearest Krispy Kreme. You'll need a humble willingness to look inward, not outward. A steady confidence in His Spirit to empower you to follow through on these resolves, regardless of how little those around you may seem compelled to follow your example.

So take a moment, right now, in the quiet of your own heart to gloat. Celebrate the sterling woman you must be to brave a book like this one, a book that demands nothing less than a radical response from anyone who reads it.

Did you do it? Good.

Now get over yourself and let's get on with it already.

There's work to be done and resolutions to be made.

My hope is that you'll read this book slowly and purposefully—not with the intention of finishing but of engaging with each segment. At the end of each chapter and section, you'll find some questions or concepts to consider, perhaps a suggested, practical application for you to implement. I encourage you to take your time, maybe even a full day between segments so you can put into practice what you're reading within the rhythms of your own life.

Again, resist the urge to "just finish." Choose instead to consider carefully where you stand with each suggestion and biblical principle, and then spend time practicing what you're resolving to implement into your life. These same questions could also be adapted for use in a small group or a regular gathering of friends, enabling you to work through these points with some sisters who can keep you accountable. That's how a resolution becomes revolutionary. Life changing.

Ultimately, our experiences together within the pages of each section will lead us to a moment of decision: the crafting of a new resolution statement. A promise. An action. A purpose to be wrapped around our lives until we are more thoroughly shaped into the image of God's will and desire. I'll ask you to read it over prayerfully—to speak it out loud—and then sign your name to it. I think it would be good, too, if you'd consider making these resolutions with your family present or with a group of godly friends who can help you (while you also help *them*) to become everything these pledges are meant to accomplish. By no means are you promising to be perfect; rather, you're making a commitment simply to begin—to journey forward in the direction each particular resolution is pointing you.

And to keep stretching for the rest of your life.

I'm confident, my fellow sister on the journey, that in this place and through these pages, your life will start to intentionally change. With God. With abandon.

Ready to do some stretching together? Me too. Let's go!

Priscilla Shirer

1. *I will embrace* my current season of life and will maximize my time in it. I will resist the urge to hurry through or circumvent any portion of my journey but will live with a spirit of gratitude and contentment.

2. *I will champion* God's model for womanhood in the face of a culture that seeks to undermine it. I will teach it to my daughters and encourage its support by my sons.

3. *I will accept and celebrate* my uniqueness, and will esteem and encourage the distinctions I admire in others.

4. *I will live* as a woman answerable to God and faithfully committed to learning and living out His Word.

5. *I will seek* to devote the best of myself, my time, and my talents to the primary roles the Lord has entrusted to me in this phase of my life.

6. *I will be* a woman who is quick to listen and slow to speak. I will care about the concerns of others and esteem them more highly than myself.

7. *I will forgive* those who have wronged me and reconcile with those I have wronged.

8. *I will not tolerate evil* influences even in the most justifiable form, in myself or my home, but will embrace and encourage a life of purity.

9. *I will pursue justice,* love mercy, and extend compassion toward others.

10. *I will be faithful* to my husband and honor him in my conduct and conversation in order to bring glory to the name of the Lord. I will aspire to be a suitable partner for him to help him reach his God-given potential.

11. *I will demonstrate* to my children how to love God with all their hearts, minds, and strength, and will train them to respect authority and live responsibly.

12. *I will cultivate* a peaceful and grace-filled life where everyone can sense God's presence not only through acts of love and service but also through the pleasant and grateful attitude with which I perform them.

13. *I will make* today's decisions with tomorrow's impact in mind. I will consider my current choices in light of those who will come after me.

Part I

THIS IS WHO I AM.

SURPRISINGLY
SATISFIED

A resolution to be content

Every Bite Counts

"This is going to be a good year for you, my friend. Thirty-six is a great age."

Thirty-six.

That's how old I was becoming and the affirmation I was receiving when I first wrote this book. It was the end of December, and my longtime friend Rachel grinned at me over celebratory coffee on my birthday. She's a decade older than me, so her brown eyes glimmered with a tinge of remembered excitement.

I'm not sure why, but something about what she said really got to me. Maybe it was just the way she said it. Maybe it was the expression in her eyes as she looked at me. Maybe it was the little smirk that curled up at the corners of her petite lips. Whatever it was, it drew me in, got my attention, and settled into my mind and heart for consideration.

"Thirty-six is a great age."

Today I'm the same age *she* was, when she said those words to me. And in hindsight, I'm even more endeared to them now than then. Because now, I get it. That's what hindsight does; it helps you "get it." Where younger eyes see challenges to be feared or fretted over, age inverts those very images of stress and uncertainty until they sparkle with all the satisfying ingredients of blessing, opportunity, and freedom.

Rachel continued by sharing some of the happenings of her twenties, the surprises that interrupted her thirties, and the settledness that had held her hand, gratefully escorting her into her forties. She'd now been married for twenty-five years, raised three incredible children, dealt with the unexpected twists and turns of life that most any person standing on the cusp of her fiftieth year has probably lived through. She'd seen disappointment, experienced incredible joy, and was now living a full life complete with deep friendships and an even deeper faith.

And here at a Christmastime restaurant table adorned with a delectable molten chocolate cake that we were ravenously sharing, she sighed the full breath of a woman satisfied. She swept her blonde bangs off her eyelids, cocked her head slightly, and told me that the season I was about to enter was a good one, that I should face it with expectation and enjoy its blessings: kids that were a bit more self-sufficient, a marriage a few years more mature, a body still pretty much pointed in a northerly direction.

Yup, recalling that year in her life made her smile. It had been good.

And with that simple comment spoken, she went back to her eating—fork to mouth dripping with chocolaty goodness.

She must not have noticed my reaction. Didn't notice the weight of her comment hitting me with a full blow, like a baseball player swinging and connecting with the pitch. With one abrupt flick of the wrist, she had sent my heart sailing into the outfield of conviction. The thing she was suggesting, implying in so many words—the way she was proposing for me to approach this next phase of life I was entering—was exactly opposite of what my proclivity had been.

I'd been the type of person, you see, whose heart and body hadn't always been good about sharing the same space. Instead of relishing each moment, each year, each opportunity, each step on the journey, I'd been constantly overeager to get to the next thing, which always looked more enticing than what was currently before me. I'd rarely been satisfied in full with my present station.

Not at thirty-six. A quick mental inventory revealed ample evidence to support the claim that I hadn't really been in attendance for large portions of my life. As a teenager, I'd impatiently rushed toward young adulthood full throttle. As a single university student, I couldn't wait to be in a committed relationship and out of college so that life could "really begin." Then with a loving mate promised for life, I enjoyed our first years of marriage, but during some of them I secretly harbored discontentment with our childlessness. And when the kids started coming, the nights were long and the days even longer, and I prayed through each of them that bedtime would come more quickly today than I'd remembered it coming the day before. I was *present* for all of those years of my life as a student, a wife, a mom—a woman—and yet there was so little I could really remember, few emotions I could recall that accompanied some of the events of life. Why? Because I'd been there, but I hadn't really *been there*.

And with my thirty-fifth year coming to a close, it occurred to me that I hadn't engaged fully in *that* year either. Oh, I'd enjoyed it for the most part, but I hadn't soaked in it, relishing it, cherishing it, celebrating it, appreciating it for what it was—the only thirty-fifth year my life would ever know. Now it was nearly over, and before me stretched another year, populated with all the things, people, events, relationships, and milestones that would make it a once-in-a-lifetime experience—my only chance to fully be the person I'd be at this age and in this season. Only for the coming year would my husband be exactly like *this*. Only for these fleeting moments would my children talk, look, and act exactly like *this*. And if I chose to hurry through in an attempt to avoid the parts I didn't like, I'd simultaneously miss all the things I *did* like about this season.

I recognized that by rushing through life, I'd been subtly devaluing those around me and the experiences I was involved in, not appreciating the importance and significance they bring to my life at this very moment, not grasping my responsibility for holding dear and treating well these gifts God has entrusted to me. Instead of embracing the privilege of being a blessing to my husband, my children, my friends, and others, I'd been quietly communicating that I wanted them to change and speed up, to get busy being somebody else, someone who's more in line with what I want and need, to hurry along to a place where they could make me happier than they currently do.

That's been me. Always looking toward the next moment, the next month, the next event, rarely allowing myself the privilege of fully participating and embracing the happenings that were right before me for that day.

And with one final bite of the most eye-opening dessert date I may have ever had, I realized this feeling had a name: *discontentment*. She shows up at the doorstep of each day eager to march inside and make herself at home. But instead of only coming for short visits on rare occasions, she refuses to leave, spreading her baggage everywhere, filling up corners of your space that you thought you'd locked up to this odious intruder. She comes, she lingers, and she robs you of your years. Then before you know it, you've missed out on the joys in the journey, the growth that comes from battling through the difficulties, the sweet and savory experience of creating the memories.

I snapped out of my momentary trance and looked down at my plate. No more full bites left. Just chocolate syrup lacing the bottom of my plate, along with tiny crumbs of spongy cake dotted with miniscule dollops of whipped cream. With new resolve I started scraping up everything I could salvage, not wanting to leave behind any part of this delicious experience. Mmmmm. It had been worth all the hard work. Tasted just as good as the first.

Glad I didn't miss anything on my plate.

And I resolved right then and there not to miss anything in my life, ever again.

- *Take a moment to savor what the Bible says about contentment:*
  - "True godliness with contentment is itself great wealth." (1 Timothy 6:6 NLT)

- "If we have food and clothing, with these we shall be content (satisfied)." (1 Timothy 6:8 AMP)
- "Make sure that your character is free from the love of money, being content with what you have; for He Himself has said, 'I will never desert you, nor will I ever forsake you.'" (Hebrews 13:5 NASB)

- *Now think about your life. What have you been hurrying through?*

- *What have you been hurrying to get to?*

- *What are some of the good parts of your experience that you've missed in your attempt to rush through the more difficult ones?*

- *What can you do differently today to "scrape the plate"—to gather up all the good things around you and begin enjoying the journey of your life?*

The Secret

When my boys were little, one of the games we liked to play was centered on secrets. Sometimes when their friends came over, we'd stand in a single-file line while the person in front whispered a secret to the one behind him. This mysterious dialogue was then passed from one to another until it reached the end. Usually, by the time it did, whatever was shared between the first two participants had become misunderstood, misinterpreted, or manipulated. Somehow the message just never got translated clearly all the way back.

The same thing has happened to us as women in this culture today. There's a secret that was first spoken and handed down centuries ago, but it sounds a lot different now. Its original message has deteriorated beyond recognition along the way, until only the most determined and discerning are able to decode it.

These days we hear a philosophy of happiness that's actually been training us for a long time to be, ironically, *not* happy. It says there's always something else, something more, some additional requirement we need before we can really enjoy life the way it was meant to be enjoyed.

So the algorithms carefully calculate our interests. And based on this gathered information, we're bombarded with advertisements and suggestions dripping with recommendations intended to whet our appetites and tantalize our taste buds, convincing us that what we already have is old and undesirable, that we simply must—we must!— acquire something new in order to be truly happy.

- *If you're single,* you should have the security of marriage.
- *If you're married,* you should have the freedom of singleness.
- *If you live in an apartment,* you should own a home by now.
- *If you own a home,* it should be bigger than the one you've got.

Getting the message?

- Your clothes should be from *this* vendor.
- Your appearance should look like *that* trend.
- Your kids should be more like *those* kids.
- Your standard of success should be measured by *these* standards.

The fallout from this is inevitable. Fed by such a steady diet of unclaimed desires, we can hardly help but develop a level of disdain for our current circumstances. Caught in this vicious cycle, we consequently feel incomplete and substandard. Unhappy. Ungrateful. Unfulfilled.

Dissatisfied.

This is precisely why a satisfied woman is such a surprising woman. She is shockingly noticeable to a world that lives on a watered-down version of the secret—a secret that this Surprisingly Satisfied woman obviously knows the truth about. You can tell it by her peace and serenity, by her solace and restfulness, by the mysterious sense of ease that accompanies her. Her presence alone delivers an air of refreshment to any setting she enters, to anyone she's around.

The rarity and uniqueness of a woman who has chosen to be satisfied with what she has, with who she is, and with where she lives is as uncommon and worth celebrating as a Texas snowfall at Christmas. She's caught the faint whisper of a secret passed down through the ages—the apostle Paul's secret: "I have learned to be content in whatever circumstances I find myself" (Philippians 4:11)—and she's chosen to trust its wisdom and to frame her life according to it, to become a woman who chooses contentment over displeasure.

Contentment wasn't some unique spiritual gift Paul had been given. It wasn't an automatic facet of his personality. It was a skill he had chosen and adopted, then had mastered and applied to his tumultuous life experience. "I have *learned* to be content."

He'd learned.

Come to realize.

Acquired the skill.

Developed the discipline.

Honed the ability.

And it all started with a "secret" (4:12), he said—a mystery that held strong and true even when his external circumstances were hardly conducive to living with a relaxed sense of well-being.

Paul was well acquainted with disappointment and lack. He'd been beaten, stoned, and hounded by his enemies. In fact, when he wrote these words in a letter to Christian believers, he was in prison facing death, enduring some of the most extreme circumstances a person can imagine. Nothing was going well for him.

He wasn't in denial. Nor was he a martyr. He readily admitted when things were bad and didn't play the persecution card, trying to draw some measure of satisfaction from publicizing what he was going through, more than everyone else.

He just knew a secret. And the secret gave him peace and serenity in the teeth of his ominous difficulties—the same secret you and I can reach out, grab, and hold on to when things are as bad as they can get, or perhaps when they're simply just not what we prefer. It's the key to unleashing a flood of joy into our hearts, the kind that rages within, no matter what is raging without.

Paul, again, had simply resolved to be content:

> *I have learned to be content in whatever circumstances*
> *I find myself. I know how to make do with little, and I know*
> *how to make do with a lot. In any and all circumstances*
> *I have learned the secret of being content—whether well fed or*

hungry, whether in abundance or in need. I am able to do all
things through him who strengthens me. (Philippians 4:11–13)

The Greek word he originally penned in verse 11 to communicate
our word *content* referred to an inner sufficiency—a satisfaction found
through the depth of one's own life with God, independent of our surroundings—the kind of emotional stability that puts women like us in
a position to be amazingly free.

When you've concluded that what you already have on hand is
enough, that it's adequate—that it's been deemed by God as sufficient—then you live from a posture of gratitude, and you're equipped
and empowered to participate fully in the tasks set before you during
this season of life. Paul described it in another place like this:

God is able to make every grace overflow to you,
so that in every way, always having everything you need,
you may excel in every good work. (2 Corinthians 9:8)

The more you believe that God's grace to you is overflowing,
the more you'll be convinced that you will always have everything
you need. And the more certain you are that you'll never lack, the
more willing and able you'll be to give of yourself and your resources
because you'll be certain God will always replenish your supply.

You can just bank on that. Your God can be trusted to grant you
the supply you need to excel at His purposes. Always.

So if you don't have it—whatever *it* is—it's because you don't need
it. You may *want* it, but it's not necessary in order to accomplish what
He knows is most important for your life today. Otherwise He'd have
given it to you. He loves you too much to "withhold the good from
those who live with integrity" (Psalm 84:11).

Whatever He's given or not given, He's done for a specific reason—
a reason known only to Him perhaps, but one you can trust with full
confidence, sight unseen. Every decision you need to make, every task
you need to accomplish, every relationship you need to navigate, every
element of daily life you need to traverse, God has already perfectly

matched up with an equivalent-to-overflowing supply of His grace. If you don't agree with that, you either lack a proper appreciation for what you have, or you are doing things that you're not supposed to be participating in right now.

You can always tell people who operate from a position of perceived lack and deficiency. They're stingy with their time. They're selfish with their resources. They're tight fisted with their energy. They're reluctant to sow of themselves into the lives of others because they're afraid they don't have enough to do it with and still have enough left over for themselves. Not enough time, energy, talent, money, skill, patience. They're like my teenage son, hoarding all the bacon at breakfast for fear it might run out.

But whenever we operate that way, the "every good work" that Paul outlines—the truly important tasks and relationships of life, the ones that promise blessing to us as well as to others—go unattended and undone. We're not able to fully participate, much less excel in something, when we don't feel like we have the proper amount, the proper brand, the proper type of resources with which to participate in the first place. So the "work" misses out on our touch, and we miss the many ways the "work" could touch us—the impact, the memories, the lessons, the experiences that God is knitting together to become a key part of our story.

God has already given enough. He always does.

And when you and I choose to recognize this and trust in His continued supply, we'll be able to engage in life in a way we never have before. We'll finally be living life to the fullest, overflowing with gratitude and contentment.

And now, sister, you know the secret. Preserve it and pass it on.

- *A woman of contentment acknowledges her needs and the resources that God has already supplied to meet them. She approaches life with gratitude for what she has, instead of being obsessed and deflated about what she doesn't. Begin*

THE RESOLUTION for WOMEN

your journey to contentment by making a list, either in the blank space at the bottom of this page or in the pages of your own journal.

My Needs | God's Provision

- *Match up your needs with the way God is currently meeting them. Then update it periodically as God continues to respond to each need. Place your list in a handy place for the times you are tempted to lean toward dissatisfaction.*

- *What might God be trying to grow in your character or cement in your relationship with Him by intentionally keeping some of your needs unmet, or at least not in the way you would prefer? How is this shaping you, and what is it teaching you about yourself? About Him?*

Overflowing Blessing

Give, and you will receive. Your gift will return to you in full—pressed down, shaken together to make room for more, running over, and poured into your lap. The amount you give will determine the amount you get back. (Luke 6:38 NLT)

Last year my friend Trina bought me a bread-making machine. The huge box came in the mail promising to deliver hot, fluffy loaves with the push of a button. I was mesmerized.

For fifteen years I'd been baking sourdough bread for my family by hand, using yeast "starter." A couple times a month, I would knead, mix, and roll dough in the hopes of giving my kids a memory that my mom gave me: the smell of homemade food in the house. But now, with this new machine promising the same tantalizing scent with a bit less work, I tore open the box, set out the machine, and opened the instruction manual.

"Use exact measurements." Emphasis on the word *exact.* Hmm, interesting. That's exactly what my previous recipe card said too. Turns out, baking bread, whether by hand or in a fancy machine, requires precision either way when it comes to the measured ingredients. No matter what else changes, apparently this facet does not.

That's because bread is moody. It has a bit of an attitude problem. You're never quite sure what sets it off, but one little bobble in the preparation process can keep the dough from rising properly or baking to a perfect golden brown. You have to be careful.

When my sons were younger, they'd pull their stools over to the counter, eager to dirty their hands in the kneading process. Before kneading, though, the flour had to be added. Six cups, to be exact. I would watch my boys carefully, knowing how "exact" those scoops must be. But over time, I was able to entrust even this step to my youngest son. He had it down to a science—a Luke 6:38 science: "a good measure—pressed down, shaken together."

He would reach the utensil down into the airtight flour bin and collect "a good measure." Nothing skimpy about the serving he gathered. Thankfully he was still holding the measuring cup over the container because flour was spilling from the sides of his scoop. But knowing the need for just the right amount to be added to the ingredients, which were already poured and waiting in a nearby bowl, his tiny fingers would secure a good grasp on the handle, and he would gently "shake" the cup. This shaking action, I'd explained to him, eliminated the air pockets that can form underneath, occupying space that can still be filled with flour. By shaking it enough, he could be sure that every square inch of measuring cup was being used for his purpose.

Finally he'd put his other hand on top of the mound and pat gently to make sure it was "pressed down." Inevitably he'd find that the cup could now hold more than before. So he continued to add flour, leveling it off until he determined it was as full as possible. Only then would he pour the scoop into the mixing bowl.

Six times he did this. Scoop, shake, press down. Scoop, shake, press down.

This, the Bible says, is how we're supposed to give of ourselves to His will for our lives. Not sparingly, not begrudgingly, but graciously and generously. And the reason we can afford to be so openhanded in our serving and blessing of others comes down to a final, additional element of our Father's biblical baking directions, an extra action He takes when He measures out His gifts to us. He does it not just with a "good measure," one that's been "pressed down" and "shaken together," but one that is "running over," where not even the brim of our needy hearts can contain it.

It appears there's nothing exact about God's recipe of return to us. His gifts are overflowing. He's not stingy with His goodness or ungenerous with His supply. He promises, when we choose to give, that He will fill us back up with even more than we had to begin with.

Now, by no means am I suggesting that you should always and without question give of yourself at the expense of the relationships and purposes that should be prioritized in your life. Sometimes the best, most empowering word you can learn to utter is *no*. But on those occasions when you do feel genuinely led by God to give, you needn't be worried about what appears to be a dwindling amount of personal resources to suit the task. If He has endorsed your involvement, you can proceed with complete contentment and willingness, knowing He will always give back far more than you ever expended. The contented woman, when required to give of her time, her love, her resources . . . herself . . . is secure in the knowledge that she possesses enough to do it. And she looks forward to experiencing the promise of an outlandish return on her investment.

I can imagine what you may be thinking because I've thought it too . . .

- My energy level is so low.
- My "love tank" is running so close to empty.
- It's only Tuesday, but my patience quota has already been used up for the week.
- My wallet is even emptier than I remember, and my financial needs aren't going away.

Yet just when you feel as though you're completely void of anything worthwhile to offer, or when your situation makes you feel justified in not being the one to participate, you'll often hear Him whispering . . .

"Give, and it will be given to you."

And when He scoops up the dividends that He'll be sending back your way, He won't be short and scanty about it. He won't skim off the excess or be bound by an "exact" measurement. He will supply you a portion that is abundantly good and beyond what is warranted. He'll shake and press, shake and press, to make sure no pockets of air are taking up space reserved for His blessing. And then He'll pile up His favor and grace into such a rounded heap that it will spill off the sides, more than you can hold. Your hands and heart will try to grasp every morsel that falls from your full container, but there will be too much coming, far too fast.

Good thing you've got a lap.

For on it will fall the abundance you cannot gather any other way, the surplus for which there is no more space. And it just keeps coming and coming.

This is the reward for the woman resolved to contentment.

So "give, and it will be given to you; a good measure—pressed down, shaken together, and running over—will be poured into your lap."

It appears that the best way to get more of what you need is to give away the little you think you have left—at the appropriate time and in the appropriate way. Yes, the best way to be Surprisingly Satisfied is to be irrationally released to respond to God's promptings to invest your life into His plans and purposes, even when doing so seems impossible because of your perceived lack.

So make the resolution—the resolution to be content. Then look toward heaven with holy anticipation, and sit with your skirt gathered up in folds and draped loosely across your lap, prepared to catch the overflow in the welcome pockets of room you've created. Live this moment. Pour yourself out. Drain the experience of each precious day. And be prepared for God's overflowing blessing.

• *When you consider your level of willingness to give of yourself, does it reveal more contentment or discontentment residing in your heart? In what way?*

- *Based on God's provisions that you listed at the end of the last chapter, what is one provision you could close this book and utilize today?*

- *Record your thoughts regarding this statement: "Sometimes the best, most empowering word you can learn to utter is no."*

- *Who is someone you could seek for wise counsel and accountability about pursuing balance in this area of your life?*

The Balancing Point

Hopefully you're beginning to see how many needs God has already met in your life that you've been discounting up until now. Yet I'm fully aware that your list of unmet wants may still be extensive as well. So possibly this clarion call to live in gratitude and satisfaction with what God has already given feels almost like admitted defeat—a resignation to the status quo, a life of mediocrity. Maybe it feels as if choosing contentment is a simultaneous choice to quell your desires and silence your future aspirations, to quit ever hoping for more.

On the contrary, contentment is the equilibrium between the enjoyment of life now and the anticipation of what is to come. Contentment serves as a guard against desires gone wild. It is the key to unlock you from the bondage of unrestrained longing that wells up within your heart and inevitably begins to control your life, making you a slave to what you *don't* have instead of a fully engaged participant with what you *do*. It is the faith-filled belief that what God has bestowed now is worthy of gratitude and appreciation, not merely because it is enough but because it is *good*.

By choosing contentment, you're not getting rid of your desires; you're just demanding that they assume an appropriate, humble position in your life, not bossing you around like a tyrannical dictator forcing you to submit to his ever-growing and ever-changing list of demands. It means you no longer allow your yearnings and aspirations to control you, to rob from you the full use of and gratitude for what you've currently been given, leaving you unable to enjoy *this* because He hasn't seen fit to give you *that*.

Making this resolution of contentment will offer you an opportunity to look forward to tomorrow with peace and ease and an appropriate level of anticipation instead of the frustration and hurriedness that often accompanies our glances toward the future. It will be your ticket to live with goals and ambitions inspired by His expansive, mind-blowing will, without having to sacrifice today's blessing.

In staying *Surprisingly Satisfied*, you actually receive the best of both worlds. You give yourself permission to enjoy fully the things you have, the person you are, and the life you're currently living while continuing to harbor the dreams that keep you growing and stretching into the future.

So the businesswoman gets to relish today's accomplishments while at the same time having high expectations for tomorrow. The homemaker learns to thrive on the joyful chaos of today's tasks while calmly, patiently looking forward to the slower pace her future may hold. The single woman is actually able to enjoy her independence—not just pretend she does—and yet be equally excited about what sharing life with a future mate may be like. She neither has to abandon hope of marriage, if that's what she desires, nor cave to depressing tinges of self-pity and emptiness.

It's a balance. A holy equilibrium. A genuine gratitude for what the day brings, all the while maintaining a controlled anticipation for what tomorrow may offer.

That's the safe, healthy place where contentment allows you to take root and take up residence. Instead of being manipulated by unrestrained discontent, instead of allowing restlessness to hustle you into decisions, relationships, and opportunities that you're unable to recognize as being faulty from the outset, contentment keeps your mind clear. Peaceful. Settled. Undisturbed. Happy to be *here*, and when God determines the time is right, happy to be *there*.

It's a resolution to be satisfied.
A resolution that will change your life.

• *Go back and reread your answers and comments from the questions in this section. Then read the resolution you are about to make. Pray about it. Sit with it a while. Rest in it. Even if you're exhausted from life's challenges and demands, make this a moment to breathe deep and savor what God is inviting you into, what He's asking you to give and what He's promising to supply you in order to do it. Talk to Him about it in prayer. Then when you're ready, make this resolution out loud, maybe even in the presence of someone who can help hold you accountable to it. Then sign your name below it.*

⚘ SURPRISINGLY SATISFIED ⚘

I will embrace my current season of life and will maximize my time in it. I will resist the urge to hurry through or circumvent any portion of my journey but will live with a spirit of gratitude and contentment.

_____

PURPOSEFULLY WOMAN

A resolution to champion
gospel-centered womanhood

Pretty in Print?

A reporter for the *New York Times Magazine* sat across from my husband and me at a local Panera Bread restaurant. And shockingly, gratefully, we were at ease.

We'd agreed to this meeting months earlier, and I'd been concerned ever since. This wasn't some local media outlet or cable-access news channel with a narrow demographic. This was the *New York Times*. "The Gray Lady." All 170 years of her. They wanted to do a story on the women's role in both the home and church, and somehow they had decided that this expanded Sunday article should feature Jerry and me as its central characters.

Seriously?

We weren't quite sure what to think about this or why they'd choose to highlight a couple like us. Sounded a bit like a possible trap—setting us up to parody as outdated relics with anachronistic viewpoints, people who had turned a blind eye to the advancements of women in the modern age. It was hard for me to imagine any scenario where this major secular news outfit wasn't going to paint our beliefs and practices as being weird and obsolete, and us along with them.

For days and weeks prior to this face-to-face meeting, I had stewed over how to prepare myself, certain that whatever I said was going to be misrepresented, misunderstood, taken out of context, written in a way that was misleading. Even as the hour approached, I braced myself for a tyrant of a reporter, antagonistic, snarling, eager to attack not only my views on being a woman in the twenty-first century but also my marriage.

So I was shocked when a pleasant, dark-haired woman arrived with a big smile, hugged me instead of shaking hands, and jumped into a conversation filled with easy, casual banter. This reporter wasn't intimidating at all. She was just a brilliant journalist and writer on the cusp of a new marriage herself, admittedly covering this story as much for the new role she was about to undertake personally as for her reporting responsibilities. I was captivated by her questions on everything from our views on Christianity, theology, and the history of women in the church to the intimate nuances of our own relationship and my take on what it means to have a biblically based view on womanhood in a hyper-feminist culture. Finding her so easy to talk with, I relaxed and settled into our conversation.

Nearly six months later the article hit newsstands. Its headline read, "Housewives of God," and it went on for eight pages with an in-depth discussion of women in general but our marriage and ministry in particular and how our belief system—a Christ-centered one, built on the husband's leadership role and the wife's position as a capable and valued partner—fleshed itself out in our home. I asserted that when lived out in the way God intended—both by men and women—this dynamic doesn't stifle or diminish; instead it provides a place for each person to flourish creatively and personally. Far from burdening me, it benefits and blesses me. In fact, it places the weight of responsibility on my husband to cultivate a safe, secure environment within which I and our children can thrive.

The reporter did a fair enough job presenting both sides of the issue as any good journalist would. People read it. And then they responded. Some in appreciation of our candor, and some concerned and alarmed that by choosing to live with viewpoints they deemed archaic, I was relegating myself, my strengths, and my gifts to a marital and theological lockbox for which only the ideals and principles of extreme female empowerment held the key to freedom.

Thus the debate ensued, fueled by numerous comments posted on social media platforms.

This clash of opinion regarding women, both single and married, is nothing new. And given the history of women's treatment in certain sectors of society, it's understandable how ideals like the ones written about in this *New York Times* article have been distorted. Both in the past and still in the present, some individuals and cultures, and some streams of the church, have mistreated, ignored, intimidated, or under-valued women, sometimes using God's Word (out of context) to support such stances of dominance, diminishment, and control. And so, if we aren't careful, the Christian woman's knee-jerk response (to *any* check on her autonomy and power) could swing so far in the opposite direction that she unknowingly abandons any semblance of Gospel-centered womanhood.

But we cannot abandon it. We won't.

Because by resolving to return to a balanced perspective on God's revelation to us in Scripture regarding our identity, we are commit-ting to honor the One who created us female and who knows us best, who has proven time and again that only in Him do we find clarity, freedom, and ultimate fulfillment in our lives. Gratefully we are benefi-ciaries of the rights and recognitions that have been hard won by cou-rageous women in history who refused to sit silently while the female gender was undervalued in society. And yet we want to balance it with our simultaneous and rightful desire to protect the venerated definition of womanhood as it's presented to us in God's Word.

If you'll look closely and objectively, you'll see that some of the principles and ideals championed through the years by women desperate to redefine and reestablish what it means to be a woman have quietly, cunningly swung the pendulum too far in one direction. Appropriate cries and appeals have, yes, led to the correction of legiti-mate injustices and low valuations of women that have *always* flown in the face of biblical teaching and the heart of God. But many of these initiatives have also robbed women of much of the uniqueness we've been created to exhibit and experience.

A Christ-centered woman—one who proudly wears the badge of womanhood given by her Father—must resolve to go against the tide. She recognizes that an accurate view of herself is impossible without an accurate view of her Creator, that the only way to truly know herself is to more accurately and fully know God and His Son, Jesus. Her identity is rooted only in *Him*, and she knows that she belongs to Him.

Her body.

Her soul.

Her spirit.

So she willingly yields to her Creator as her ultimate authority, and she champions His design and definition for women. Then she embraces, accepts, and experiences its boundaries and its blessings.

Because God's ways are good.

They are *all* good.

You, God's woman, are a paradox—a potent mixture of strength and vulnerability. Powerful yet tender. More than capable, yet willing to yield. You are smart, wise, equal in worth to men, and secure in yourself as you relate to others, yet content to surrender yourself to your Creator's authority. You do not strive for acceptance or approval because you know your value is not tied to your relationship status or achievements.

You are a woman whose lifestyle inspires other women to live fully and abundantly, drawing them toward the God who makes a woman so rich, deep, and captivating.

Your identity is not in question. It has been defined and established by the Creator of all.

I realize your stage may not be the *New York Times*. Very likely mine will never be again either. But we are all on a platform every day, a position entrusted to us each morning when we swing our legs out of bed. From atop this daily rostrum, you and I remain constantly in the spotlight, where the life we've resolved to live will either champion or demote the beauty of biblical womanhood. We will compel our daughters either to desire it or to fight against it. We will encourage our sons either to appreciate it or to take advantage of it.

Yes, this platform has been entrusted to us. As a result, an audience of friends, family, loved ones, children, coworkers, and social media followers are all watching not only to see how we live but to ascertain our attitude as we live it.

What kind of woman are you going to be?

Your answer is at the heart of this resolution.

- *How have you seen our culture's distorted view of womanhood most clearly exhibited?*

- *How do you see young women being enticed away from biblical womanhood?*

- *What biblical principles of womanhood strike you as stifling or repressive? Why do you think you feel that way?*

- *As you continue to read, offer your concerns about this issue to the Lord in prayer. Ask Him to use this time to answer your concerns and reaffirm His priorities for you in this area.*

It's Good to Be a Girl

I recall watching a news program that talked about how agnostics know as much or more about God as religious people do. You never know exactly what to make of studies and statistics like these, but researchers apparently stood outside a church service of some kind and asked the people coming out to name the first four books of the New Testament. Many couldn't.

Shocking, right?

Or is it?

Our knowledge of God and His Word is sadly waning, especially since commitment to church participation, in far too many people's eyes, is increasingly not viewed as seminal to their spiritual growth. Yet in few places is this deficiency of biblical literacy more noticeable than in how we view the true definition and value of womanhood. As women, we need to know it in order to live it out. And men need to know it too, in order to rightfully honor us as women even as we honor them. In a culture inundated with many illegitimate ideals that have skewed and distorted identity, the only possible way for us to live out and champion a truly Christ-driven perspective is if we are aware of what it entails, including God's intention and design in creating us.

At the root of the feminist movement—and still one of the concerns of our modern culture—is the unequal treatment and valuation of men and women. And rightfully so. It is a great injustice when women are minimized based on their gender. From the very beginning, the inherent dignity of the female gender is specifically addressed in Scripture. "God created man in His own image. . . . He created them male and female" (Genesis 1:27). Translation: *men AND women are both created in God's likeness.* You, as a woman, are worth neither less nor more than your male counterparts. You are different, obviously, but only in function (which I'll address in the next chapter), not in value.

Centuries of human history testify to how this God-given truth has become twisted into inappropriate ideas and labels, which some societal and religious structures have parlayed into abuse and subjugation. The false perception that an inequality of *value* exists between men and women—as seen, for example, in significant salary differences in the workforce—has caused many women to be overlooked or ignored.

But you, sister, are not only an equal partner in the created order; you have been called "good" by God Himself—"very good," in fact (v. 31).

Not just good but *necessary.* Adam alone couldn't accomplish the tasks assigned to mankind by the Creator. Man was in need of a partner. Without her, these endeavors would go undone.

So from the beginning, God placed a mark of importance on women and their contributions. They were (1) *good* because they bore His image and (2) *necessary* in the achievement of His purposes on earth.

Look around you at the sphere of influence the Lord has placed you within. This circle of people and circumstances is in need of *you.* The touch, experience, wisdom, and feminine heart you bring into these arenas are all required if that sphere is to be what He has purposed it to be. You are not an addendum, a last-minute afterthought that can be tossed out without notice. Without your participation and input, much will be lacking.

Yet with humanity's fall into sin and the decay of the human condition, women soon became downgraded and relegated to obscure, second-rate status, valued almost entirely on the basis of their relation to other people—as the wife of their husband, for example, as the mother of their children, and nothing more. Throughout the annals of the Old Testament, we see women often failing to be treasured, prized, and cherished as the Creator had intended them to be.

Enter Jesus. With the coming of the Messiah in the New Testament, God reaffirmed the significance of women through the life of Christ, who countered a culture that demoted women's importance and value. He exemplified instead, in the flesh, the true heart of God.

The fourth chapter of John's Gospel highlights just one of many remarkable occasions when Christ demonstrated His regard for women and their inherent value. The arrival of a Samaritan woman at a local well where Jesus happened to be sitting presented an extreme problem. For starters, traditional ancient Jewish culture didn't allow for friendly exchanges between Samaritans and Jews. In addition, and in an even larger context, first-century men didn't enter into conversation with women in public, not even their own wives. So for Jesus to be found speaking to this woman, asking for a drink of water, was not only culturally inappropriate but would've been readily perceived by onlookers as scandalous. More than just a breach of protocol, it was shocking. Disgraceful.

But this is Jesus we're talking about—a revolutionary who never sought to fit comfortably within societal norms but rather to stand against them, to change them, and to present a new world order both to that particular generation and every successive generation that followed.

So, He did. He not only engaged her in casual conversation but invited her opinions on theological issues that men of His historical age would never have expected a mere woman to be capable of entertaining. Despite rabbinical condescension and a nearly unanimous cultural disdain for women, Jesus treated her like a person, a person of intelligence, someone who mattered, someone who was as worthy of the Messiah's "living water" (v. 10) as anyone else. In His mercy and love, He extended to her a gift of which most all others would have deemed her undeserving: His grace, His covering . . . Himself . . . to cleanse her, keep her, and sustain her.

Truly Jesus left no doubt in His dealings with this divinely appointed individual that women are both *important* and *worthy*, as well as fully qualified to be *entrusted*. For not only did He bestow on her the gift of His salvation, but He also entrusted her with His message to share with others. After her encounter with Christ at a community well, she returned home telling everyone what had happened to her, urging them to come see for themselves. The result? "Many Samaritans from that town believed in Him because of what the woman said" (v. 39).

A woman . . .

Good.

Necessary.

Important.

Worthy.

Entrusted.

Being a woman was never a curse to be endured or a gender to be tolerated. It is a gift to be treasured and esteemed. It is God's chosen way for us to relate to Him as Creator and Father and to demonstrate, along with men, the unfolding love story of Christ's relationship with His people (Ephesians 5:22–31). It is our special way of experiencing Him and His love for us in a harsh, critical, deconstructive world. And it is our gift to our generation and the world in which we live.

Lo and behold, it's a privilege to be a girl.

• *Choose one of the many roles you currently play in your life, and record for each one how you are . . .*

- good for it
- necessary to it
- an important component of it
- worthy to be a part of it
- entrusted to fulfill your role in it

- *In what situations and around which people have you found your value or dignity most challenged and questioned? How do these experiences affect you?*

- *How can we raise daughters who will understand their value apart from their achievements, relationship status, or acceptance by peers? How do we raise boys to view women with a similarly high regard? Discuss with friends some creative approaches.*

Role Reversal

In June 2021, my husband and I dropped off our oldest son, Jackson, at college. He'd been scouted and recruited to play football at one of the leading Division I universities in the country and had gotten a full tuition scholarship to boot. Given all the upheaval and uncertainty of the previous year (multiple pandemics—medical, racial, and political), we were elated and grateful to the Lord for His intervention and provision.

After six weeks of arduous, early morning workouts, as well as a painstaking weightlifting program and meticulous nutrition plan, he FaceTimed us to say he'd packed on ten additional pounds of pure muscle to his already solid six-foot, two-inch frame. He now weighed in at a whopping 255! I was stunned. The boy was a giant to begin with, but now . . . *now!* . . . he was giant-er.

Was that even possible?

College athletes are big. In many cases, much bigger than my freshman son. Huge, bulking muscles. Incredible speed. They demonstrate more strength and athleticism in one afternoon of work than most of us could generate in a lifetime.

And yet as formidable as these guys are, they are not the most powerful people on the field when they suit up to play. I always get a kick out of the other men out there—many of them much smaller, older, and balding, each in their striped black-and-white shirts, standing in the midst of these gargantuans, tossing their yellow flags and blowing their whistles.

Referees are not anywhere near the size of the athletes they share a playing surface with. And yet at every single one of their commands, directives, or decrees, the game comes to a halt. Burly men who outweigh them by perhaps more than a hundred pounds apiece (and perhaps make a lot more money than them too!) stop what they're doing and follow their instructions.

They choose to *yield*.

Imagine how difficult and unmanageable the game would become if they didn't.

This demonstrates an important aspect of biblical womanhood that needs to be refocused and brought back into balance. Because if we really intend to hold to this resolution, championing God's view of womanhood, we must recognize that His creation entails not only an inherent feminine esteem but also an established order. Human relationships are not designed to be a raw contest of power and strength but rather a self-restraint empowered by the Holy Spirit. Therefore, we exert our greatest influence in life by knowing how to harness our God-given strength so that we align with His created order.

We do it by making the Spirit-led, mutually beneficial decision to yield to authority.

It's critical to emphasize this isn't just a married woman's directive. Submission is for both men *and* women, single *and* married. It is a universal principle by which we all flourish. According to Scripture . . .

- The employee, whether male or female, must submit to his or her employer (Colossians 3:22).
- The citizen, whether male or female, must submit to the governmental authority (1 Peter 2:13).
- The believer, whether male or female, must submit to spiritual authority (1 Peter 5:5).
- The child, whether male or female, must submit to the parent (Ephesians 6:1).

- And, yes, the wife must submit to the leadership of her husband (and here's the key portion of this verse) "as to the Lord" (Ephesians 5:22–23).

Hear me clearly. This "as to the Lord" means biblical submission does not call us to follow any person blindly and without question. Your submission and mine is "to the Lord," so that by walking within these divinely ordained roles of submission to legitimate authority, we place ourselves inside His protective covering, where blessing can spread in all directions, and where everyone can experience the freedom that His truth—and His truth alone—is designed to offer. Infringe on these boundaries, however, and we're looking for trouble. It's just that simple.

Order *matters*—whether we understand it or agree with it or even want it. Nothing can truly and ultimately be enjoyed when we're not willing to remain within boundaries He has outlined.

Throughout the first wave of the feminist movement, which began during the nineteenth and early twentieth centuries, as well as the second major wave in the 1960s and the subsequent iterations that have followed, the basis for each initiative has been a clamoring for rights. And while many of these rights have been worth defending, we must be careful as Christian women to prioritize our most powerful right of all: the right to yield with willingness and dignity to the One who created us and to those men and women who represent appropriate and healthy leadership for us.

A woman's strength—the true strength of *any* person, for that matter—is not only seen in the demonstration of her power but in her willingness to yield herself, her will, her body, and her ambitions to her Creator's design for her. Only by surrendering to His intention for womanhood in every area of our lives will we as women ever experience the liberation we are trying so desperately to recover elsewhere.

No doubt, sister, you are powerful and capable in your own right, perhaps even *more* capable and competent than some of those to whom you're called to submit. You are gifted and necessary—indispensable—one who bears the image of God Himself. And yet all of that strength coursing through your nature and personality will only thrive and be its best as you yield to the legitimate authority established by God. The key word here being, *legitimate.*

Remember, this is true for men as well. True for everybody. Like the professional athlete who could easily overpower the referee, or the child who has become more adept at a particular skill than her parent, or the employee who may honestly be more proactive than his boss, or the wife who has a more expressive personality or a higher pay grade than her husband, each must still respect the position the established leader has been allocated.

Even the most powerful Man ever to walk the earth demonstrated the importance of this principle:

> *Though he was God, [Jesus] did not think of equality with God as something to cling to. Instead, he gave up his divine privileges; he took the humble position of a slave and was born as a human being. When he appeared in human form, he humbled himself in obedience to God and died a criminal's death on a cross. (Philippians 2:6–8 NLT)*

If One so great could display this level of humility in order to achieve a much, much greater result, then what excuse do we have for not choosing to do the same?

I believe that much of the frustration we experience in our lives— much of the frustration I've experienced in mine—is directly linked to our refusal to yield to God's design regarding submission. Like a fire that is best enjoyed within the confines of a fireplace, your strength can best be displayed, its benefits most fully experienced, when you choose the trusted, effective boundaries of God's established order.

This is the essence of submission. A necessary ingredient for both biblical manhood *and* biblical womanhood—a necessary ingredient for any disciple of Christ.

Often this concept sends a chill down our spine, even to the strongest of us. Maybe that's how it strikes you as well, given the way someone in your life has distorted and misused the principle. Choosing to submit may feel to you like you're automatically relegating yourself to inferior status. But this is not the way God intended it to be, and I encourage you to seek out godly advice from those who can help you navigate your specific situation with wisdom. Yet we cannot throw the baby out with the proverbial bath water just because it's gotten dirtied by misuse.

Your Creator infused such great worth into you, too much to then demean you into subservience by His own design. Why would Jesus, one of the most highly respected and powerful men even in the eyes of unbelievers, choose to live a totally submitted lifestyle—one He described in this way: "I always do what pleases [the Father]" (John 8:29)—if it wasn't the best choice for living?

Surrendering to submission is meant to provide a framework in which your potential can truly flourish.

It is not akin to waving a hypothetical white flag, diminishing yourself or folding to some lesser way of living that demeans and devalues your talents and gifts. It doesn't relegate you to a narrow lane of effectiveness or lessen your contribution.

Could it do that? Yes.

Historically it's been unjustly used to subjugate whole people groups. So, yes, it could. Not all leaders live their responsibilities well. Perhaps, if you're married, your husband doesn't. And both you and your family reel from the difficulties that spring from that, to one degree or another. Your husband, like any leader in God's created order, will be held accountable for how wisely, how carefully, how devotedly, and how biblically he has handled his role.

But, sister, so will you.

Since your ultimate submission is to your Creator, ask the Lord (and a wise friend) to show you how you can still respect your husband while remembering you are never called to submit to anyone who leads you into sin or is abusive toward you. If you are in a marriage where your conscience and safety are under threat, whether physically or emotionally, the duty of submission does not call you to endure any demand without question. Hear me? Make no mistake about that. But also think honestly about how often your resistance to another's lead is a mere matter of opinion and preference, a refusal to do *anyone's* bidding just because your own perspectives differ?

As we've explored before, submission is something every disciple—man or woman—is called to do in some form or fashion. But the question for you and me isn't how it's going for everybody else. Nor is it how everybody else is getting it wrong. The question for you and me is how it's going for *us*. In our lives as women. As single women and wives alike. As sisters and citizens and friends. How is submission going for *you*?

Our fallen inclination is much like Peter's, who cried out: "Lord, what about him?" We want to know God will sort out the next person's issues before we'll obey Him in our own issues. And the answer of Jesus remains the same: "What is that to you? As for you, follow me!" (John 21:21–22). Will you wait to obey until everyone else does? Or will you obey the Lord in your own life and womanhood right now?

So prayerfully consider these truths regarding this aspect of biblical womanhood, and seek wisdom on your specific circumstances in light of all you've read here. Ask yourself some questions like:

- Are you offended at the thought of yielding to the authority of another?
- If you are married, is this something you rebel against?
- If you are single and dating, have you considered the importance of this aspect of marriage? Is he committed to *his own* submission to God, and does he make himself accountable to legitimate earthly authority? Trust me, you'll want to make sure of it before you say "I do."
- Are you even now pursuing a spiritual covering by seeking accountability with those who've modeled a submitted life to the Lord, those whose godly maturity can provide you with strong, helpful counsel and direction as you navigate life?
- Are there any ways in which you've allowed the misuse of this principle by some to stir in you a resentment for it or to negate it altogether?

A place of freedom and peace awaits every woman who aligns herself with God's design. It's up to us to expose the lies of our age and to remind this generation of the true beauty and value of the submitted woman.

This is our resolution.

• *In preparation for signing your second resolution, read this statement again: "A woman's strength is best seen not in the demonstration of her power but in the yielding of herself to God." Consider it carefully and determine what it will look like when fleshed out in your own life. Make this resolution with confidence, knowing that you are choosing to align yourself under His all-wise plans. Enter with freedom and sign your name to signify your commitment.*

❧ PURPOSEFULLY WOMAN ❧

I will champion God's model for womanhood in the face of a culture that seeks to undermine it. I will teach it to my daughters and encourage its support by my sons.

_____

AUTHENTICALLY ME

*A resolution to value myself
and celebrate others*

Intelligent Design

Four years ago, we moved from the small house we'd lived in while our children were in elementary school. It was a casually styled three-bedroom home on a couple acres of land in a rural suburb of Dallas. Nothing elaborate or fancy. My boys shared one small bedroom and we homeschooled in the other. It was livable and cozy. The beauty of nature often beckoned us outdoors to chase butterflies, fish at the neighbor's pond, or take turns on the tire swing.

My sister and her family lived next door. She has three boys too, who are the same ages as mine. So on any given day, all six of them would run between houses, bursting in and out of the screen doors, glistening with sweat and panting from their fast-paced childhood activity.

This is the way we both wanted to raise our boys in those formative years, without pretense and posh. We wanted them to be *boys* through and through. That's why I never filled that home with expensive, delicate furniture. Too many dirty hands and noses around to keep up with that. Instead, I bought some moderately priced, practical pieces in dark sustainable colors that I knew could weather the man-child hurricane of our lives and hide the stains that would come with it. I loved the sturdy sofa and kitchen table that survived those elementary years.

Which is why when we first viewed the new home that would eventually become ours, I had trouble warming up to it. It didn't fit our old furniture. This new house called for a different style and, more specifically, different-sized furniture pieces. My old amber-colored sectional, for instance, was ill-fitting for the new living room space, which had a more modern color scheme, taller ceilings, longer dimensions, and more elegant moldings. The rectangle, dark wood kitchen table I adored wasn't suited to the square breakfast nook and the uniquely tiled floor. A couple other casual leather chairs we owned were the wrong size and style to work into this more upscale, refined space. So, at first, without even considering more important, foundational questions like the size, location, or quality of the house itself and how well it was suited to our family's changing needs, I immediately discounted it. Because shouldn't we buy a new house that could accommodate our beloved old stuff?

My husband though, thankfully, helped me snap out of this imbalanced perspective with one simple yet poignant question: "Are you really going to base such a big, important decision on such small, inconsequential details?"

I didn't need to answer. Not out loud anyway. His point was clear.

There were bigger, more substantial things I should've been considering first. A decorating dilemma shouldn't be my chief litmus test. As comfortable and familiar as these nostalgic pieces of furniture were, they weren't supposed to dictate the course of my next move—a move that would matter in our quality of life for years to come.

Unfortunately, I can look back and point to other times when I've had this same skewed thinking in life. I've often allowed illegitimate criteria to determine how I navigate different seasons of my life. For example, sometimes I've allowed the sum total of my self-worth and identity to be based on an inconsequential detail that should really have had no bearing on my sense of value and dignity.

Like the span of my hips or the texture of my hair.

The approval of peers or the acceptance of a certain social group.

Past mistakes I've made or difficulties I've endured.

Society's redefinition of what it means to achieve success.

I shouldn't let these kinds of things have the final call on the type of woman I am becoming.

Again and again, in more ways than I'd like to admit, I've let the menial, the inconsequential, the trivial, even the totally false and inappropriate, keep me from making sound, rational, balanced decisions about how I choose to live this one life God has given me.

Maybe you've done this too.

Maybe you've picked up bits and pieces of false, worldly ideology or other skewed philosophies on identity, gender, or sexuality, and then slowly, almost imperceptibly, changed your perspectives (and ultimately yourself) to match.

Maybe you've acquired one or more distorted cultural paradigms and suggestions along the way that you've felt pressure to embody instead of believing you're enough just the way you are.

Or maybe you've blown certain things out of proportion, like an isolated event or a momentary setback, then basically allowed it to identify you, forcing you to build the rest of your life around it. Before you knew it, you were being controlled by something that honestly shouldn't have the clout to boss you around. Now you're maneuvering your whole life to accommodate a circumstance or idea that you'd given far too much rope in the first place.

It's unbalanced. Backwards. Absurd. Out of order.

There are bigger, more sweeping decisions we need to make first. Truths we need to believe and align our lives around. Not minor bells and whistles but foundational things. Structural things. Unchanging, divinely ordained realities we need for gauging our decisions and directions.

And that's why this resolution is so important to me, to you—this commitment to assign genuine value to who we are, based on our God-given worth, talents, gifts, and abilities. Because once we've settled this issue—this main issue—everything else can begin falling appropriately into place. We'll be inspired to get rid of ill-fitting things and acquire the courage to replace them with the "furniture" that's better suited to this new direction in life.

The life you're moving into has far too much God-given potential for you to enter it still clinging to old habits, limitations, attitudes, and assumptions. Dig deep and lean in to the truth—the truth of who you are and what He's created you to offer to the world—and then orbit your life around that steadfast knowledge.

- *What are some minor incidentals you've allowed to have too much bearing on your future?*

- *Outside of God's truth, what have you allowed to shape your self-image or self-worth?*

- *In the past, how have you tried to force old things (habits, mind-sets, people) into the new spaces God is moving you into?*

- *Read 1 Peter 2:9–10 and record the statements of value declared concerning you. Make a point of really studying and meditating on this Scripture, digging more deeply into the truths revealed.*

Supernatural Selection

Recently I watched a world-renowned celebrity being interviewed. She looked as beautiful as always. Charming and dignified. Her toffee brown skin was like smooth, buttery silk draped perfectly over a toned, lean, statuesque body. She was a sight to behold. Every bit the prominent, accomplished, acclaimed public figure we've all seen on the stage of her profession.

And yet even this woman—admired by millions, rewarded with great wealth and social status—said something I really didn't expect. Responding to one of the interviewer's questions, she answered, "I've never had a very healthy self-esteem. I don't even know how a person gets that. I'm desperately trying to figure out where to find it."

Huh? Her? Not happy with who she is? I was shocked. A woman with so much talent and prestige, now in her mid-fifties, having known little other than position and prominence her whole adult life, revealing an inner struggle she'd battled for years and years—the longtime attempt to discover, enjoy, and celebrate herself.

We know from revelations like this, just as we know from our own struggles with the same kinds of feelings, that our true, lasting value must be based on something besides the visible and exterior.

Not just *something* else but *Someone* else.

Hear it explained in the Father's own voice as He speaks to a young man who'd similarly lost touch with a healthy self-concept. Seeking to encourage the young prophet Jeremiah, God said to him . . .

*I chose you before I formed you in the womb; I set
you apart before you were born. I appointed you
a prophet to the nations. (Jeremiah 1:5)*

Read that verse again. Hear those three staggering declarations with the ears of a daughter listening attentively to the voice of her loving Father.

"I chose you."

"I set you apart."

"I appointed you."

This is truly who you are. A woman *chosen*. A woman *set apart*. A woman *appointed*. You are not here by accident at this moment with this book in your hands, along with an accompanying desire to make some serious resolutions that will reshape your whole life. It is no mistake that you are living right now with your own set of circumstances, dealing with your specific set of issues, all while working within your personalized set of skills and abilities.

God has made you *you* and has placed you here. On purpose.

1. *He chose you.* You are involved in a divinely designed, carefully calculated, and eternally significant plan. For reasons you may not fully understand or even agree with, God selected you as His own. This was not a quick, halfhearted decision on His part. It was a deliberate, volitional act of God Himself, made with thoughtful consideration and wisdom.

Choosing, as it is used in this verse, denotes a knowing. His choice of you was based on a deep, intimate knowledge of who you are: who you are now and who you are becoming in Him. So even if you simply cannot fathom why God would choose a person like you to participate in a particular activity, He Himself is well aware of His reasons. He has selected you, and everything about you, to participate in the work He is doing at this point in history. Like a coach who methodically considers which runner to put on the track at particular stages of a relay race, God's choice of you for this leg of the marathon was by design.

That's why you're here. In *this* position.

Facing *that* project.

Married to *that* man.

Involved in *that* friendship.

Dealing with *that* issue.

Living in *that* neighborhood.

Spearheading *that* committee.

Participating in *that* activity.

Mothering *those* children.

Influencing *that* group.

Living *this* life.

Not because it has accidentally happened like this but because you have been known and chosen by the one Coach who sees you as uniquely suited, equipped, and capable of carrying out His plans with intricate precision.

You are the one, my friend.

You. Are. The. One.

This overwhelming realization is what brought my friend Anna to her knees one day, releasing such a steady stream of warm, worshipful tears down her pretty face that they soon began dripping from her chin. She'd recently been rejected . . . again. This was her second broken engagement, the final straw that had broken whatever thin, tiny shreds of self-worth were still left in her heart. You can imagine. She felt (and believed she had every reason to feel) unloved, unappreciated, undervalued. In her estimation, little of herself was redeemable or attractive enough to make her worth another's attention. Not any more. Not after all of this. Who needs to be shown more than twice—in perhaps the most humiliating, most personal, most vulnerable way possible—that nobody wants you?

But Jesus' words to His disciples, to her, to us—just like God's words to Jeremiah—stunned her with their power and peace: "You did not choose me, but I *chose you*" (John 15:16). She'd seen that phrase in Scripture before but never like this—not with the glowing highlighter of God's Spirit hovering over it, punctuating each word with the pinpoint precision of divine clarity. *I chose you.* The words rested on Anna's heart like a soothing balm, covering the gaping wounds, refreshing the dry landscape of her soul. With this phrase began a new journey of realization for her, the same revealed discovery that each of us must hear and receive and welcome inside if we're ever to live out the plans He has for us. Your value, like mine, is ultimately found in the undeserved but wholly divine selection processes of God.

2. *He set you apart.* You're not like all the other relay runners. If you spend all your time looking at the runner behind you or focusing on the one ahead of you, wishing you had their skills and talents, your lane will go unattended. We don't need the same runners. We need each unique runner. Runners who have been set apart for their particular tasks, fulfilling their own roles, running their particular leg of the race in this time, in this place.

Being "set apart" carries the idea of being dedicated for a specific use at a specific time, being reserved for those opportunities when (and how and where) you can best be used, when you can most be yourself. It's like the special dishes you might keep in your china cabinet. Maybe you received them as a wedding gift. Most of the time they're kept behind glass, looking out onto the kitchen table in the other room where the everyday plates and cups get to have all the fun. But when those key moments come around, the ones that call for a special touch, only the fine dishes will do.

You are a holy vessel of God, set aside for specific times when the uniqueness you offer can be fully used and valued—"a special instrument, set apart, useful to the Master" (2 Timothy 2:21). He has blessed you in Christ "with every spiritual blessing in the heavens" (Ephesians 1:3), freeing you to engage fully in the life He has called you to lead, in ways He is faithful to reveal to you as you walk closely with Him.

A young writer recently e-mailed me, expressing concern because she didn't think her style of writing had enough depth and intrigue. She mentioned several other authors she admired, people she wished her writing was more comparable to. "If it were," she said, "I might actually be able to finish this project I've been working on." As I read her sentiments, I thought about how I frequently feel that same way—wishing I had more depth or creativity like I've admired in someone else. And yet others have had to remind me of the same thing that I wrote back to this young lady: some readers will only hear, understand, and accept certain things when they read it in *your* words, from *your* perspective, written in *your* voice. We were each created by God to do *our* part. And if we fail to do it because we don't think it's valuable enough, great loss will be suffered. Someone, somewhere, needs *you*—in all of your uniqueness—to step into the lane of your calling.

So come take your place. Embrace your special role. Enjoy the thrill of capitalizing on your strengths and surrendering your weaknesses without wallowing in misery over your lacks and differences or allowing yourself to feel threatened by those traits you should be celebrating in those you admire. You are not a mistake, no mere outcome of happenstance. Your creation was supernaturally superintended by Almighty God. You are extraordinarily significant.

Rather than seeking to impress and outperform others, and rather than feeling ashamed by what you don't have and can't do, relish the opportunity to stand as a living, walking, breathing example of what God's grace can do with a woman He has set apart, limitations and all, to be a sacred vessel in His service. You are a purposeful place setting. A masterpiece worth celebrating.

Nothing commonplace about that.

3. *He has appointed you.* Being chosen and set apart is quite an honor, but make no mistake—it comes with great responsibility. Among the reasons God chose you (or as another Bible translation says it, "planted you"), one was to put you in a position to yield specific outcomes in your personal life situation. Jesus finished the thought like this: "You did not choose Me, but I chose you. I appointed you to go and produce fruit" (John 15:16).

Therefore, you can trust that He has planted you right now in the place where you will be the most personally productive. Even if you may not be inherently pleased with the person He's made you to be, even if you may not be abundantly happy with the circumstances you're currently living, you can be sure that God has planted you here with design and intention. He has selected the "soil" where you're presently growing. Every kind of season and weather you experience has had to pass through His fingers before coming into contact with you. It's all been divinely designed to surround you with the conditions that allow your unique gifts and abilities to reach maximum potential. To grow. To yield. To produce.

And like any farmer, He expects to reap what He's sown. Apple seeds are supposed to grow apple trees. Radish seeds are supposed to grow radishes. Likewise, your seeds are designed to produce a crop that's uniquely yours. So there's no point in trying to produce fruit that is someone else's to grow. Your job at any given moment is to bring all your gifts, all your talents, all your propensities, and all your passions into this thing called life and believe they are good enough to produce the fruit that is expected of you.

Trust Him. He knows you. He has special plans for you.

I don't know all the things you're struggling with at this moment as you strive to attain a healthier self-image. But I know that the only way to see yourself more clearly is by seeing *Him* more clearly. The better you know Him, the more you can rest in the genuine, authentic reality of your value in your Creator's eyes—the One who chose you, set you apart, and appointed you to bear fruit. He has loved you enough to make you like no other, and He's given you a task that is yours alone to complete with His abundant help and empowerment.

Resolve to love being you, the way He loved creating you.

- *Choose at least one of the following verses to study and memorize:*
  - Ephesians 2:10—a declaration of your importance to God
  - Jeremiah 1:5—a confirmation of your selection by God
  - 2 Corinthians 3:5—a verification of your sufficiency in God

- *Consider the things you may have opted out of doing (or even trying to do) because you felt ill-equipped or unworthy to participate. Choose one of them to begin doing this week.*

Happy to Be You

Instagram wasn't a thing when I published the first draft of this book. It had only launched the year before and was slowly gaining steam. I didn't know much about it and had no intention of using it at the time. Wasn't even sure what it was, not until several years later when I opened my own account and started posting.

Now a decade later, Instagram is my main form of communication and presence on social media. Throughout the day, I scroll through it to be inspired by people I don't know and kept up to date on many of the ones I do. I'm often intrigued at the precision and intentionality that many users invest on their images and captions. The videos are edited exactly, the photos are staged and lit impeccably, and the lives that each post represents look doggone near perfect, with layers of filtering slathered on top. Makes for fun and engaging viewing for sure, but I've noticed it also creates a unreachable standard that becomes an unspoken goal to achieve and maintain. All of a sudden, the unfiltered, natural version of us doesn't seem to be enough. The more we look in on others' lives, the more uncomfortable we can become just being us.

The *authentic* unfiltered version of us.

If we're not careful, we'll spend so much of our lives wishing or pretending we were somebody different from who we are that we'll never get to experience the sheer freedom of just being ourselves.

If we're not vigilant, we'll spend so many years and put so much effort into being "liked" and steering clear of our own uniqueness, we wouldn't know our true self if we bumped into her face-to-face.

But rediscovering and celebrating the *you* that God originally created is paramount for any woman who desires to live out her primary purpose.

You are the only *you* the world has. The only one we really need. The one who, according to Psalm 139, has been . . .

- examined by God.
- known by Him.
- seen by Him.
- protected by Him.
- followed by Him.
- blessed by Him.
- guided by Him.
- strengthened by Him.
- supported by Him.
- carefully created by Him.
- led by Him.

Have you ever really tried getting acquainted with this person who was important enough to God Himself to put this much time and attention into creating and supporting? When you strip away the façades and remove the veneers, when you take off any masks and remove any pretense or disguise, what's left is the authentic person who is precious in the sight of God Himself—fully capable and distinctively designed to achieve His purposes for her life.

You. Just the way you were meant to be.

So take time to uncover and reconnect with these things that truly describe you: your gifts, talents, passions, eccentricities, dislikes, weaknesses, interests, and uniquenesses—in their rawest, most unspoiled form. Don't rush through this. Peeling back the stereotypes and labels, the misinterpretations and stigmas you've used (both knowingly and unknowingly) to define yourself will probably require some time and effort on your part. And choosing to move forward in authenticity will require even more. In fact, you might even need to enlist the help of a few close friends to assist you.

First, ask them to point out, from their own perspective, what makes you unique. It's often more difficult to see yourself as clearly as another person can who's close to you. Beauty tends to become familiar. Genius eventually feels commonplace. You get used to yourself. You overlook the astounding, remarkable aspects that make you uniquely special because you've grown so accustomed to having them. Your rarity becomes unremarkable when it's just another part of your regular routine.

So open yourself to hearing someone remind you what they see in you. Write these things down. Internalize them. Accept them. Your gifts and skills. Your personality and temperament. The things that make you noticeably, singularly you. Your strengths and, yes, your weaknesses.

Second, pinpoint what ways (if any) that you have neglected to use or celebrate these characteristics, and become intentional about honoring your uniqueness in the future. Think what a wonderful gift this return to authenticity could be to you over the years, even over the next few weeks. Being able to live in genuine freedom, unburdened from the harried exhaustion of making impressions or trying to act like somebody you're not. No longer overcompensating for things that have kept you feeling like you don't measure up. Aligning yourself with God's will instead of constantly fighting His plans and always working at cross-purposes.

Accepting yourself.

Treasuring the value He's encased within you.

It's a resolution worth making.

• *Record uniquenesses other people see and value in you. Which of these are the most surprising to you?*

• *Record how you can be more intentional about using and celebrating these characteristics.*

• *How would the dynamics of your family, your office, or your relationships benefit from your doing this?*

The Affirmation Crusade

My husband is fascinated, intrigued, yet still somewhat bemused by the fairer sex. He's discovered a plethora of feminine dynamics in the years we've been married that he admits he'll never fully understand. Like, for instance, why a weekend trip requires packing more than one pair of shoes. Or why the mere act of talking could ever be such an enjoyable hobby. He's asked me lots of questions over our twenty-three years together, hoping to figure out some of these things. And yet even after my fine attempts at explanation, he tends to just smile, pat me lovingly on the cheek, and then walk out the door shaking his head in disbelief.

I guess a man will just never understand some things that are crystal clear to a woman.

Perhaps none more than this: the powerful effect of a compliment given from one woman to another.

He heard me telling a girlfriend not long ago that the skirt she was wearing really accentuated her pretty legs. He heard me tell another that her hair was "just lovely" in that color and style. He's seen other women come up to me, expressing gratitude for a particular personality trait or just to tell me that the blouse I was wearing was really cute.

And for the life of him, he doesn't see how this works. Men just don't do this, he tells me. Never, for example, will I ever catch him praising another guy's hair, or telling a friend how that button-up really brings out the broadness in his shoulders. "That's just not something we do," he says.

But it is something we do, my sister friend. Something we ought to do a lot more often. Cancel culture is loud; *affirmation* culture should be louder.

We are relational in a way most men are not. We thrive on our friendships with women and appreciate the commendation we receive from them. There's something about another woman's admiration that we can accept more fully because, for the most part, we're certain no strings are attached. No ulterior motives are underneath it. Just an honest, encouraging assertion expressed by another.

And while our self-worth should never depend on others' compliments or approval, we experience a certain depth of blessing when we are affirmed by other women. While appreciation from men is flattering, a sister's compliment carries a purity, simplicity, and gentle strength that refreshes us. It helps us feel reassured, supported, and warmly comfortable. Plus it does something else, something powerful; it diffuses any need for competition.

When you take seriously this resolution—this decision truly to accept yourself and your uniqueness—you'll finally be comfortable offering the same favor of acceptance to those around you. You'll be free of the time-consuming frustration of seeking to fit others into your own personal set of expectations. You'll allow them to be themselves. And as an added bonus, you'll be better able to enjoy celebrating and commending their exceptionality—the things they can do much better than you—because you'll be so completely comfortable with yourself and your own distinct capabilities. Their excellence will inspire you instead of threatening you.

This third resolution not only affects *you*. It will also enhance the women around you as they experience the affirmation that bubbles up from the security you're living in. This should be our mandate, our campaign. A movement of women linked by our resolution and devoted to seeing it manifested in the lives of the women around us.

It can be our crusade.

Our *affirmation* crusade.
Our gift, one sister to another.

• *Take time to look back over your notes from this section. Consider what will be required for you to live authentically, as well as the freedom you'll experience when you do. Additionally, think of some other women who, for whatever reason, you are hesitant to compliment. Make a point to commend them for their unique value and worth to you this week. Read the resolution out loud and sign your name below it.*

❧ AUTHENTICALLY ME ❧

I will accept and celebrate my uniqueness, and will esteem and encourage the distinctions I admire in others.

———————————————

FAITHFULLY HIS

A resolution to be devoted to Christ and defined by His Word

Divine Appointments

My heart has heard you say, "Come and talk with me." And
my heart responds, "Lord, I am coming." (Psalm 27:8 NLT)

The Susan B. Anthony dollar was minted in 1979 by the United States government and again in 1999. It was the first circulated coin to bear the image of a woman. Its goal was to celebrate the advances of women and the impact our gender has made on the country as a whole.

Only one problem. This silver coin looked nearly the same as a quarter, which often caused people to confuse the two. The value of the coins was significantly different, but their appearance was remarkably similar. Therefore, the Susan B. Anthony dollar just didn't catch on with the public, and circulation was eventually discontinued.

You, sister, have been "minted" in the likeness of God and have been called "out of darkness into His marvelous light" (1 Peter 2:9). As His daughter, you should never be lost among the shuffle of worldliness—whole dollars confused among a handful of quarters—driven by lowly pursuits and interests, becoming so similar in appearance to everyone else that you can't be singled out in a crowd. Christ has placed great worth, value, and dignity on you as His daughter, fellow heir to a divine "inheritance in the saints" (Ephesians 1:18). You have been invested with gifts, talents, and uniqueness that God Himself deemed you suitable to carry. You are . . .

Surprisingly Satisfied.

Purposefully Woman.

Authentically You.

But that's not all. You also have the opportunity to be . . .

Faithfully His.

Clearly, the investment of this much godly treasure into one person's life carries with it a responsibility you and I should consider a privilege to respond to. He deserves our resolve to faithfully and consistently live up to the value we've been given, to portray outwardly to the world the inherent worth we possess inwardly by God's sacrificial yet freely given grace. Our goal should be to take responsibility for our actions and, by the Spirit's empowerment, line them up singularly with our God and His Word, diving deep into the divine purposes for which we have been placed on earth.

This is the resolution of the woman who is *faithfully His.*

- We are women who lean into His voice—listening, heeding, conforming our will to His.
- We are women who uphold the laurels of Scripture in the face of contrary opinions.
- We are women who do not ultimately answer to earthly authorities but to the One who created us, loved us, and called us to Himself.
- We are women who live with heaven's purpose in view and heaven's whisper in our souls.
- We are in the world, but we are not *of* the world—not controlled by it, consumed by it, compelled by it.
- We are heaven called, pursuing His purposes and driven by the passions He has placed within our hearts.

This is what makes us different. Unique. In the face of a culture that is blatantly turning against God, we will be faithful to Him and the trusted wisdom of His Word. The author of Hebrews noted an unexpected example of this kind of faithfulness:

Therefore, holy brothers, who share in the heavenly calling,
fix your thoughts on Jesus, the apostle and high priest
whom we confess. He was faithful to the one who appointed him,
just as Moses was faithful in all God's house. (Hebrews 3:1–2 NIV)

Excuse me? Moses? Faithful? Really?

That's sure not the way it seems when you take a quick glance at his early years—and by "early," I mean eighty or more. Raised as the prince of Egypt, he was forced to run for his life after brutally murdering one of his countrymen. Throughout the next forty years, he lived in much less than desirable circumstances, tending sheep—a job well below his pay grade and educational level. God startled him one day by speaking to him from a burning bush, commissioning him to a far more prestigious position: leading Israel out of bondage. But when called to the job, Moses spouted nothing but excuses as to why he couldn't fulfill the role. When he finally did comply and accept God's directive—after some mighty patient arm-twisting on the Almighty's part—he was often known to lose his own patience with the fickleness of the Israelite people and allow his anger to get the best of him. In the end Moses' disobedience to the Lord's instruction would cost him final entrance into God's chosen land for His people.

So . . .

If I'd been the author of the book of Hebrews, I'm not sure Moses would've been my first choice for an illustration. And yet this writer singled him out, describing him as "faithful in all God's house."

If Moses had been alive to read this verse, I wonder what his reaction might have been. He possibly would have recalled all the debacles and errors he'd made along the road of life, shaking his head in embarrassed disbelief, wondering if this author was lucid when he'd penned that text. Maybe a good case for what *unfaithfulness* looks like but—recalling how he'd lived—certainly not *faithfulness*. Come on.

Can you relate to that? Maybe your eyes meet our fourth resolution with that same disheartenment. So many blunders and mistakes stand out. So many lapses in judgment. How could you ever live up to this standard of being distinctly devoted, utterly separate, a person "faithful in all God's house"?

That's why Moses' example should give you and me great hope and encouragement. For despite his lengthy record of inadequacy, something about his story, legacy, and heritage was deemed worthy of highlighting and repeating. And tucked inside these simple verses from Hebrews 3 is the crucial, deciding theme upon which Moses' entire story hinges.

The key was in the calling.

It was "heavenly" (v. 1).

In spite of all kinds of spills and sputters in the execution, Moses held fast to the calling the Lord had placed on his life. "He was faithful to the one who *appointed* him" (v. 2 NIV). Even in the noisy wind tunnel of guilt and regret, even with loud music inviting him to dance with the decadent, he could still catch the faint whisper of heaven compelling him to forsake temporary feelings and pursuits for the sake of God's will. And herein lies what separated him and his people from all others.

He was not perfect, but he was purposeful.

He wasn't without mistake, but he was marked by God's presence.

He marched to a higher standard, an overriding and compelling force that drew him to desire what mattered to his God more than what mattered to other people. An overarching view of his life reveals a man not swayed by the whims and fleeting passions that sought to redirect his focus from heaven's call. He was headed to Canaan. His goal was milk and honey. And even when it meant picking himself up off the deck of defeat and discouragement, he did not stop until God Himself allowed him to go no farther. He was called by heaven—an appointment that ordered his priorities, pursuits, and passions. Not perfectly but persistently.

Faithfully.

We, too, like Moses, are privileged to share a calling that has heavenly origin. Even now, if you listen closely, you can hear its echo in your heart—can't you?—inviting you to go on an adventure with God. As you turn these pages, look inward to see if you're sensing an inner gnawing for something *more* to be experienced in this life of yours. If the potential of these resolutions causes your heart to burn with holy anticipation, then you are experiencing the call of heaven—inviting you, beckoning you, encouraging you. Yes, heaven is calling out, looking for the faithful who will not only wake up each day listening for it but will respond to it when they hear it. It's this groaning, this soul cry that longs for things eternal, not for the things of this world. Whole dollars, not fractions. It's what causes us to feel a bit unsettled, sensing an internal ache we're never quite able to quell, one that will not allow us to find complete satisfaction in the silver coins of culture's currency.

God in Christ has made us different, and now He invites us to desire the things He made us different for. This is what qualifies the faithful—those who recognize, accept, and pursue God's path, knowing He will see to it that His calling comes to fruition. The "faithful" are those who resolve to prioritize and pursue the divine mission given specifically and uniquely by the Father, as opposed to the pathways of earthly success and social approval.

It's why the social media influencer would choose to use her platform to unashamedly laud her faith despite the followers and endorsements she might lose as a result of her boldness.

Heaven calling.

It's what causes a single woman to refuse the offer of a distinguished gentleman who's got everything going for him except a passion for spiritual things and an interest in God's plan for her life.

Heaven calling.

It's what compels a ministry leader to keep moving forward with her study and planning and the building of God's "house" even when finances and even when her hard work is not appearing to pay off.

Heaven calling.

It's what keeps a wife faithful to her marriage, compelling her to forsake all others and prayerfully pursue the best in her marriage.

Heaven calling.

It's the call of the faithful. You and me. To fix our eyes on Him and His plans for us, and then—with the empowerment of the Spirit—to go about achieving them in our various relationships and endeavors.

What do you sense heaven is calling you to do and be? What do you believe to be God's overarching purpose for creating you and then setting you down in this generation at this particular point in history? Do you know? Are you seeking to discover it as you wake up in the morning listening for the hush of heaven? The best way to begin is by being faithful to what He has set before you right now. Sense the stirring in your soul as God's Spirit quickens you to see what He's called you to do today. Then pursue it at the expense of all else.

Unashamedly.

Diligently.

Faithfully.

Shhhhh. Listen.

Heaven's calling.

• *How is Moses' example encouraging and inspiring to you?*

• *How will you be required to go against rationale or cultural pressure to stay committed to what heaven is calling you to do in this season of your life?*

Faith vs. Faithfulness

For you know that the testing of your faith produces steadfastness.
(James 1:3 ESV)

The years leading up to 2020 were difficult for my immediate family. Within a short span of time, we endured a steady stream of loss that stirred an unfamiliar grief in us all. The spiral began with the sudden, completely unexpected loss of my thirty-eight-year-old cousin, Wynter. We were all still reeling from the shock of her death when an aunt, two uncles, another cousin, grandfather, mother, and mother-in-law all passed away within the months that followed over the next two years.

Devastating.

During this season of our lives, we all leaned on one another to find respite, encouragement, and comfort. And, as a daughter, I saw my own father in a new light. Dad has always been a tower of strength—preaching truth and living it out consistently in his daily life. But things were different now. He'd experienced heartbreak at every turn, barely able to catch his breath before the waves of difficulty rolled back in again. The majority of the family members we'd lost were directly connected to him—his niece, his sister, his brother, his father, and one month later, his wife. Truth be told, until then I'd only seen my father cry on two occasions that I can remember. But within those two years I lost count. I now expected to see dampness touch the corners of his eyes more than not.

But here's what I noticed through the disappointment and discouragement and unsettledness and heartbreak and mounting grief of those seemingly unending and unbearable days. Dad was steady. Yes, he cried. We all did. He dealt with uncertainty. We all did. But he and his actions showed us how to live within the holy tension of *asking God questions* without *questioning God*. Daddy continued to laud the character of God and stand firmly on the promises of God even as he waded through the disappointment regarding his own circumstances. He prayed honestly and authentically, voicing his heartfelt sentiment to the Father and asking the hard questions to which He desperately sought divine answers. But through it all, He did not (nor would he allow us, his children) to call God's character, power, or sovereign plans into question.

Dad demonstrated to me the essence of . . . *faithfulness*.

And I am forever grateful.

Faithfulness isn't the comfortable, untested summary of someone's beliefs. That's a person's faith. Faithfulness is instead the physical outworking of his or her actions over time and through challenge. It's more than just having a firm persuasion; it's moving that firm persuasion into forward motion. Having a strong set of beliefs is one thing. But standing up tall on them, making decisions according to them, and adjusting your life to line up with them—especially when life is unreasonably tough—that's quite another.

That's faithfulness.

Faithfulness is born when the outward expressions of your beliefs are lived out over time. Often through difficulty. For difficulty is where faithfulness is honed and brought to life. You'd never classify someone as being faithful unless you'd seen her stand firm during a course of action and decision where it would have been much simpler to throw in the towel. Faithfulness is demonstrated in consistency, steadfastness, and Holy Spirit-empowered perseverance.

It would be a real waste of time, for example, if you and I were to spend all these pages and pages of time together, sign our resolutions, believe in the impact we expect them to have on us, then close the cover and go about our lives as if we'd never made any decisions at all. We would be, in essence, like someone who trained all winter to run a half-marathon in the spring, then on the weekend of the race, got talked into going to the beach. We can *believe* that these resolutions would be effective, but if we don't act on them, we'll never see the fruit they were designed to produce. We'll never fly on the wings of God's Spirit. Never experience the places His Word gives us access to.

Making resolutions is not what will make us faithful, any more than being nestled in a carefully built nest can make an eaglet fly. Only when the mother bird stirs the nest, making it uncomfortable for her beloved babies, does the eaglet finally spread its wings, push out into the unknown, and keep going until it reaches the destination. Faithfulness is born out of this discomfort. It's the fortification that enables you to stay in flight no matter how much muscle and determination it takes to keep your wings flapping. This is what makes us faithful.

Faithful to heaven's call.

Like Jesus. During His life and ministry here on earth, "he learned obedience from what he suffered" (Hebrews 5:8). Though He always had a firm persuasion to seek His Father's will and was perfectly successful in doing so, He *proved* His faithfulness by working it out day by day, living through difficulties, surrendering His will (Luke 22:42), offering prayers and petitions (Hebrews 5:7), and staying committed to His Father's purposes regardless of His own human desire to steer away from crucifixion and death. As a result, "he was perfected [made complete], he became the source of eternal salvation for all who obey him, and he was declared by God a high priest" (vv. 9–10)—prepared for His ultimate purpose because He'd "learned obedience" the hard way. Walking against the grain. Stacking up His bold profession against the bitter perils of life. Staying completely surrendered, totally committed to the Father's plan. Not just for a day but over a lifetime.

Faithful.

And if this is something that even Christ—deity clothed in humanity, our ultimate example of holiness and righteousness—if even He chose to humble Himself enough to prove His faithfulness through experience, then the same is certainly true of us.

Hopefully you're a person of faith. But heaven is calling you to be a person of *faithfulness* as well. When you're at your job. When you're hanging out with friends. When you're struggling financially. When you're faced with a tough decision. When you're doing your daily life and wish you were doing somebody else's. By resolving to be *Faithfully His*, you are deciding to allow everything you believe about God and His Word to consistently guide your feet, your hands, your mind, your heart—despite anything and everything that may point to the contrary.

In a world marked by constant change and incredulous options, a woman who is resolved to live faithfully is an irony. A mystery. But being different is worth the cost of being diligent and strong. Being uncharacteristic is worth the cost of feeling complete and lacking nothing, prepared by God for the great work He has for her.

For you.

His faithful one.

- *In your own words describe the difference between having faith and being faithful.*

- *Would you describe yourself as a faithful person? If so, in what areas of life?*

I'd Like a Word with You

The Bible. We treasure it, and yet like too many valuable things in our lives, we have a tendency to turn it into just another burden. We often think of reading it as something we've "got to do"—usually something we "haven't done."

It's easy for us to begin feeling this way about His Word unless we realize that being *Faithfully His* is rooted in the kind of relationship we have with Him through the Scriptures. He has given us His Word to learn from and enjoy. To refresh us. To call out the desire for relationship with Him that He's planted deep within our souls. To speak to our hearts. To show us who He is. To awaken us to our failings, yes, but then to draw us toward the restorative, redemptive blessings of obedience. Not only that, but like a radiation treatment on a cancerous cell, His Word is actively renovating us even when it seems like nothing remarkable is taking place.

His Word is not a chore. Not a nag.

It's life. It's love. It's truth, solid as a rock.

And it's not just to read. It's to absorb. To bathe in. To live by.

To inspire us, reshape us, and define us.

That's because it's alive. Not simply a book written with historical data for your information but animated by His Spirit for your edification—to speak intimately and personally to you regarding His purposes for your life. If you'll listen closely as you read it, you'll feel the warmth of God's breath brushing across your cheek as His Spirit infuses old words with right-this-minute application. Most often, heaven's call to you will be heard as you are soaking in His Word. And your ability to remain steadfast in your pursuit of the "faithful" label will germinate from the encouragement you receive through its precepts. Since faithfulness is a fruit of God's Spirit (Galatians 5:22), you can be certain that His Spirit within you will work in tandem with the edification you receive from remaining consistent in His Word, helping you press on toward the goal—"the prize promised by God's heavenly call in Christ Jesus" (Philippians 3:14).

So as I've worked on the updates and revisions that I wanted to include in this section on being *Faithfully His*, I was certain the remainder of this chapter needed to remain the same way it's always been. But interestingly enough, ten years ago, this section is the one I received the most negative feedback about. People thought it was a cop-out for me to simply fill pages with Scriptures instead of penning my own thoughts, insights, and paragraphs. Some warmed to this chapter while others skipped it entirely since it was "just back-to-back verses."

But these next few pages carry the heart and soul of every resolution you'll make and the power you'll need for carrying it out. So I can't bring myself to change it. It would be a disservice to you (and to me). Without a personal commitment to prioritize and engage God's Word, you'll lose your way and your strength. The Bible is the tool divinely inspired to guide and equip you for a life lived faithfully. In a world inundated with ideas to the contrary, it is your constant reminder of who you really are, why you're really here, and who you really belong to.

You're His. And His Word helps to keep you sure of that.

That's why I want to give you this lengthy list of affirmation statements taken directly from the Word of the living God. They're not direct quotes from Scripture, but they recast the theme of the referenced verse so you can declare it in first person. These are not necessarily to be read all at once. I hope you'll return here again and again, years into the future, just to read a half dozen or so at a time, keeping yourself grounded in who you are, whose you are, and what this glorious, eternal, triumphant fact means to you.

As you *audibly* speak these biblical statements over your life and the lives of your loved ones, your mind will be renewed, your faith strengthened, your actions and attitudes transformed. "Faith comes from what is heard, and what is heard comes through the message about Christ."

- I love the Lord my God with my whole heart, soul, and mind (Mark 12:30).
- I walk by faith and not by sight (2 Corinthians 5:7).
- The Lord is on my side. I will not fear what man can do to me (Psalm 118:6).
- I am competent not in my own abilities but because He has made me competent by His Spirit (2 Corinthians 3:5–6).
- I abide in Christ, He abides in me, and I bear much fruit (John 15:5).
- I have the mind of Christ; therefore I act in a way that is consistent with His actions (1 Corinthians 2:16).
- He will never leave me or forsake me (Hebrews 13:5).
- I do not look with disdain upon my weaknesses. I see them as opportunities for God to display His powerful strength and grace through me (2 Corinthians 12:10).
- No weapon formed against me can prosper, and every tongue that rises up against me in judgment will be condemned (Isaiah 54:17).
- I will be hospitable without complaint (1 Peter 4:9).
- I will not use my tongue to speak cursings, but rather I will speak life-giving blessings to everyone I meet and in every situation I face (James 3:8–10).
- The Spirit indwells me; therefore I am the temple of the living God (2 Corinthians 6:16).
- I am faithful over a few things, and I will be made ruler over many (Matthew 25:23).
- I humbly submit to God, and I actively resist the work of the devil, knowing he must flee from me (James 4:7).

- I will not give the enemy an opportunity or foothold in my life (Ephesians 4:27).
- The One who is in me is greater than he that is in the world (1 John 4:4).
- I choose to obey the Lord and receive the prosperous abundance and blessing He will bestow on me (Deuteronomy 30:8–9).
- My heart keeps the commandments of God. They will add length of days and peace to my life (Proverbs 3:1–2).
- I walk by the Spirit and do not fulfill the desires of my flesh (Galatians 5:16).
- I am enabled to exhibit the fruit of the Spirit: love, joy, peace, patience, kindness, goodness, faithfulness, gentleness, and self-control (Galatians 5:22–23).
- The Lord guards my going out and my coming in, today and forever (Psalm 121:8).
- I rejoice in the Lord whether circumstances are good or bad (Philippians 4:4).
- I will not be afraid when I lie down, and my sleep shall be sweet (Proverbs 3:24).
- I obtain the favor of the Lord (Proverbs 12:2).
- The Lord is in my midst, and He sings over me with joy (Zephaniah 3:17).
- I am the apple of my Father's eye (Deuteronomy 32:10).
- Goodness and mercy will follow me not only today but all the days of my life (Psalm 23:6).
- I have been made in the image and likeness of God Himself. This is my heritage (Genesis 1:27).
- I have not been given the spirit of this world; rather, I have the Spirit of God that I might know the mind and will of God for me (1 Corinthians 2:12).
- I am not ashamed of the gospel of Christ (Romans 1:16).
- My steps have been ordained and ordered by the Lord (Psalm 37:23).

- I only allow my mind to entertain what is honorable, right, pure, lovely, noble, excellent, and worthy of praise (Philippians 4:8).
- I long for the pure milk of the Word that I may grow to spiritual maturity (1 Peter 2:2).
- I seek peace and pursue it (Psalm 34:14).
- I am a necessary and useful part of the body of Christ, and I will use my spiritual gifts to edify others (1 Corinthians 12:7).
- Faith, hope, and love—especially love—abide in me (1 Corinthians 13:13).
- I am the righteousness of God in Christ Jesus (2 Corinthians 5:21).
- I have been given victory in Christ Jesus (1 Corinthians 15:57).
- I am meek, and I will inherit the earth (Matthew 5:5).
- I extend mercy to others, and I will in turn receive mercy (Matthew 5:7).
- I have a pure heart before God, and I expect to see His manifest presence in my life (Matthew 5:8).
- I discipline myself for the purpose of godliness since it holds promise for the present life as well as the life to come (1 Timothy 4:8).
- My ambition is to be pleasing to Him and Him alone (2 Corinthians 5:9).
- I do not judge fellow believers so that I will not bring judgment on myself (Romans 2:1).
- My priority is to seek first the kingdom and God's righteousness, and I expect all needed, secondary things to be added unto me (Matthew 6:33).
- I am a true worshipper. I worship in spirit and in truth (John 4:23).
- I do not live by bread alone but by every word that proceeds from the mouth of God (Deuteronomy 8:3).
- Rivers of living water flow out of my inner being (John 7:38).

- I have been chosen by God to bring forth fruit that shall remain (John 15:16).
- I am a brand-new person. My old sin nature has passed away, and everything has become new (2 Corinthians 5:17).
- No matter my past, I am forgiven of my sins because of the lavishness of His grace upon me (Ephesians 1:7).
- I have been given every spiritual blessing in heavenly places (Ephesians 1:3).
- Because He was wounded, I am healed (Isaiah 53:5).
- In Christ, I am whole and complete, lacking nothing (James 1:4).
- Whatever I ask for in prayer according to the Father's will, I believe that I have received it (Mark 11:24).
- I am part of a chosen generation, a royal priesthood, and a holy nation. I am one of God's own people (1 Peter 2:9).
- I will not be afraid because I know the spirit of fear is not from Him. He has given me a spirit of power, love, and a sound mind (2 Timothy 1:7).
- I am not a stranger to God. I am a citizen of God's kingdom and a member of His household (Ephesians 2:19).
- I have been sealed by the Holy Spirit who indwells me. He is a pledge from the Father of my coming inheritance (Ephesians 1:13–14).
- I am a masterpiece created in Christ Jesus in order to walk in the good works He has prepared for me to do (Ephesians 2:10).
- For freedom I have been made free. I walk daily in this gift of freedom (Galatians 5:1).
- I am dead to the power of sin (Romans 6:11).
- I have been raised with Christ, and I sit with Him in heavenly places (Ephesians 2:6).
- I am the salt of the earth and the light of the world (Matthew 5:13–14).
- I will not fear because the Lord is my light, my salvation, and the strength of my life (Psalm 27:1).
- The joy of the Lord is my strength (Nehemiah 8:10).

- I trust completely in the Lord; therefore I will be like a fruit-bearing tree that continually finds nourishment despite dry, parched weather (Jeremiah 17:7–8).
- No good thing will the Lord withhold from me as I walk uprightly before Him (Psalm 84:11).
- Jesus Christ is my Lord and Savior, and I will do the works that He did (John 14:12).
- In Christ I have become a child of God, and I receive the blessings God has for me (John 1:2; Romans 16:17).
- In Christ, God has chosen me as His own and made me strong. He has placed His mark on me. He has placed His Spirit in my heart as a guarantee for all He has promised (2 Corinthians 1:21–22).
- I can do all things through Christ who strengthens me (Philippians 4:13).

- *Today God invites you to live a life marked by faithfulness. This is an attainable goal for you by His Spirit and with the guidance and encouragement of His Word. No matter what your past has held, this resolution can mark a new beginning. Read the resolution prayerfully and sign your name to it when you are ready.*

❧ FAITHFULLY HIS ☙

I will live as a woman answerable to God and faithfully committed to learning and living out His Word.

_____

Part II

THIS IS WHAT I HAVE.

MY BEST

A resolution to devote myself completely to
God's priorities for my life

Boxes

I knocked softly on the door of Jill Briscoe's hotel room—a woman I'd long admired from a distance, one I was thrilled for the chance to spend time with after I'd discovered we were both scheduled to speak at the same conference. She was nearly seventy years old at the time and had been actively involved in ministry for decades. She'd cultivated a long marriage and raised her children. And I—a young wife and new mom in the fledgling stages of ministry—was feeling a bit strained in this season of life: the feeding schedules and diaper changes, the wakeful nights and early mornings, topped off by the responsibilities of a growing ministry. I was tired. Overwhelmed. Out of sorts and out of balance.

I needed a dose of her wisdom and perspective.

Stealing little moments like this was something I'd gotten in the habit of doing—seeking out women whose lives swayed to the cadence of God's grace, people who shimmered with the joy of His presence, capturing the opportunity to snag one or two scraps of wisdom from their conversation. As I sat cross-legged on the floor of her hotel room, expecting nothing in particular but everything at the same time, I knew if I'd just listen, I'd glean a few nuggets of ageless truth to take away with me.

Speaking in her delicate British accent, she whisked me on a journey through her early years, revealing some of the lessons she'd learned along the way, as well as the ones she wished she'd learned a lot sooner. Each time I asked her another question, I'd lean in, chin in my hands, elbows on my knees, listening for her thoughtful answers. Not a single one failed to make an impression. In the eighteen years since that conversation, so many of them have stuck with me.

Especially the one about the boxes.

No, she didn't pull them out from under her bed or fish them from a hiding place in the closet. She simply painted them in my imagination and then set them out before me, one beside another. Clear, glass boxes, each with a lid on top that opened and closed from a hinge fastened to the side. All were exactly the same size, and each was filled to the same level with a clear, bluish, water-like substance.

"These boxes, Priscilla, are symbolic of the activities of one's life, the various undertakings into which we must invest our time, talent, and energy. Our tendency is to try keeping them just this way—equally filled with identical amounts of our energy, time, and effort. This, we think, is what balance looks like.

"But in reality, this is the picture of a woman overworked, frustrated, and exhausted. A life *out* of balance.

"The way we achieve balance, my dear, is to consider prayerfully God's priorities for us in the current season of life where we're situated, and then rearrange the boxes accordingly—pushing some of them into the background, bringing others to the front. Into these primary boxes we place the best of ourselves and our effort, while leaving the others unattended—at least temporarily—not because they're of any less overall significance but because they're not where we need to be allocating the best of our abilities and attention for the time being.

"Balance is not when the boxes are equally filled but when we are free to fill only those that are important for now, without feeling guilt over the ones that we've left for another time and place. This is balance, little sister. Remember it."

I have.

And the lessons learned from the boxes have saved my life.

- *If you have a tendency to spread yourself too thinly, in what kind of state does this typically tend to leave you at the end of the day or the start of a new week?*

- *Using the boxes below, ask the Lord what priority each one should represent in this season of your life. (Add more if you need to.) Which of them need to be moved to the foreground, and which ones need to be pushed to the background for now? Shade each one to indicate the level of time and effort you invest. Compare them and prayerfully consider if your priorities reflect God's intentions for you right now.*

Timing Is Everything

I think we all know what it means to give our best (because you've probably already been doing it)—pursuing excellence, pressing ahead even when you feel like giving up and getting lazy, making the necessary sacrifices that keep you on point and on task. You're likely getting exhausted just *thinking* about a resolution that has anything to do with giving more than you already are. And sure, we're going to talk about that a bit—giving your best instead of halfhearted leftovers—but I think you'll be surprised to find that by the end of this section, you won't feel like you're responsible for doing more. Rather, you get to do less.

So don't get so hung up on the "giving the best of myself" part that you don't get to the other part—the part that changes the playing field of this resolution: getting clarity on your "primary roles." We can't benefit from our understanding of one without having perspective about the other. If you do your best, for example, but you invest much of it in the wrong things, you've not only wasted a lot of your energy and resources; you've also lost time and opportunities you may never recover. Achieving clarity on both halves of this resolution equation is essential.

Being your best at what *God* wants you to be doing—that's the thing to shoot for.

This balancing act took center stage during the latter part of the Old Testament, after a remnant of the Hebrews had returned to their native homeland from exile. The Lord spoke to them through the prophet Haggai, questioning the priorities they were demonstrating. The order in which they were choosing to rebuild both their nation and their lives was off-kilter. While the temple lay in ruins and disrepair, the people were spending considerable time and resources on the rebuilding of their own lavish dwellings.

"These people say: The time has not come for the house of the LORD to be rebuilt." The word of the LORD came through the prophet Haggai: "Is it a time for you yourselves to live in your paneled houses, while this house lies in ruins?" (Haggai 1:2–4)

Imagine for a minute what it must have been like for these people, straggling back into a geographical area that had been ravaged decades earlier by marauding forces. The many tasks of cleanup and debris removal, the restoration of even a primitive form of infrastructure, the cultivation of arable farmland—they faced it all. All at once. The land was in need of everything.

On top of these physical requirements, they were likely feeling an incredible release of pent-up emotions, having been held for years against their will as a subjugated people group in a foreign land. This chance to start fresh—despite the many challenges of reclaiming a land gone to seed—must have come with an intoxicating sense of excitement as they sought to reestablish their own little corner of the world.

So I think we can all admit—their desire to give time and attention to the rebuilding of their own homes was understandable. It was even honorable. Why then did God express such concern?

Turns out, He wasn't concerned with what they were doing as much as *when* they were choosing to get it done. See if you can detect the pattern:

- "This people say, 'The *time* has not come . . .'"
- ". . . even the *time* for the house of the LORD to be rebuilt."

- "Is it *time* for you yourselves to dwell in paneled houses while this house lies desolate?" (vv. 3–4 NASB)

Rebuilding the destroyed temple (and thereby restoring the worship of God to a place of prominence in their lives) was obviously of greater priority to Him at *that particular moment* than construction of their elaborate dwellings. He wasn't saying their homes didn't matter. He didn't mean they should be ashamed of themselves for taking any thought about their own shelter and living arrangements. But the time for concentrating their efforts on their own houses was for later, not for now. Now was the season to focus on the house of God, to pare down their list and concentrate primarily on what God was telling them to do today. So, yes, it meant that something which brought them pleasure would need to be put on the shelf *for now* but certainly not forever. They were to focus on today's task, pushing others to the side temporarily, while being assured that the *time* would come for them to prioritize another thing later on.

Sometimes this realization can be a hard one. One friend of mine realized that she was spending an inappropriate amount of time helping her extended family (an admirable task), which was taking away from the attention she should have been paying to her own immediate family. She loves her parents and siblings dearly, of course, but after solving their problems, bearing their burdens, listening to their issues, and taking care of their concerns, she couldn't help noticing that she was emotionally and physically depleted. God's Spirit began to challenge her to consider that now was not the time (and she was not the savior) to handle the concerns of her extended family at this level of investment. In order to engage fully in God's goals for her in this season, she had to perform a difficult but essential restructuring of her priorities. Challenging but necessary.

As you're able to determine what your current priorities should be, and as you're obedient in setting other things aside for the time being, don't fret that you'll never again have the opportunity to spend time pursuing them. The next years, perhaps even the next few months, will bring with them a recalibration of what's most pressing and important.

Then some of these activities that you've needed to shutter for a time may be ready again to emerge into active duty.

Until then, fight the urge to spread yourself too thin.

Home in on what matters today.

When my children were small, my alignment of priorities looked different from that of a retired grandmother. And it should have. A college student's primary concerns for this season of her life will look different from those of a new graduate seeking to begin her career. And it should. Whatever moment you're living in will cue you toward the responsibilities that are inherent for you in this time and space.

So do *those*.

Focus on *those*.

Give yourself permission to say no to certain things that are not in alignment with these priorities right now. And force yourself to delay certain things that aren't your primary mission for this moment. In doing so, you'll find that every yes comes with a lot more freedom and fulfillment.

• *Ask a wise, honest friend who knows you well how she thinks you're managing your current priorities.*

• *As you think about those things you want to do but can never seem to make time for, remember the biblical appeal that says, "There is a time for everything, and a season for every activity under the heavens" (Ecclesiastes 3:1 NIV). How could this deliberate act of trust and perspective free you to invest yourself more joyfully in today?*

Anything, Everything, and Whatever

So, whether you eat or drink, or whatever you do,
do everything for the glory of God. (1 Corinthians 10:31)

"Whatever you do . . ."

One of the richest blessings that comes from making the tough decisions we've been talking about in this section—decisions to shift some things into the background for this season of life so you can focus on what currently matters more—is that it unlocks your ability to finally do things well, to do them in a way that magnifies and honors God. Perhaps like many women, you constantly feel like you're failing. You end most days with the sense that you're inadequate, that you don't have what it takes, that you just don't have it together like everybody else seems to.

This burden is especially heavy for the perfectionist. She's often paralyzed because her standards are at such an impossible height. She has so much to do and such a high bar set for herself, she's discouraged before she even begins trying to reach them all. She can't do *anything* well because she's exhausted from trying to do *everything* perfectly. She looks at all the half done and undone tasks around her and melts into despair. Perfection is a surefire way to live in shame and guilt your entire life, never satisfied with yourself or your surroundings.

So just to be clear, this resolve to offer the best of yourself is not a call to perfectionism. In passages like Matthew 5:48, where Jesus instructs us to "be perfect . . . as your heavenly Father is perfect," He's not saying that He expects you to live without a single flaw or bobble. You are being invited into a life of *wholeness* and *completeness*. That's what the biblical word *perfect* means. It's not a standard of faultless accuracy and precision but rather an invitation to devote the whole of yourself—your time and your talents—toward the *completion* of the tasks He's appointed.

This resolution is actually encouraging you in the *opposite* direction of perfectionism. It's encouraging you to relax, accept your limitations, cut back, and primarily engage in those activities that your loving Father has set before you in this season of your life. Most likely you don't have a poor work ethic or bad character. You're just allowing yourself to be pulled in too many different directions. As a wise friend once said to me, "Priscilla, you cannot do a thousand things to the glory of God, but you can do one or two." And though she said it in jest while observing my crammed schedule and scattered priorities, her sentiments still hold true. When you choose to do *everything*, you can't do *anything* well. But when honoring God is your one thing, it pares down your purpose and narrows your focus.

And for the record, doing things well is something *you can do*!

The Bible promises it.

Why else would Paul admonish us to accept his "whatever you do" encouragement as a living reality—not just once, in 1 Corinthians 10:31, but again in Colossians 3:17: "Whatever you do, in word or in deed, do everything in the name of the Lord Jesus, giving thanks to God the Father through Him"?

He said it because it's true. If you and I will take the time to zero in on our unique, divinely given set of "whatever you do" qualities (as I encouraged you to do with your *Authentically Me* resolution) and then commit to bring them wholeheartedly to the tasks the Lord has given us, He will help us not only accomplish those tasks sufficiently but also in a way that brings Him glory. Trying to do what someone else has been commissioned to do will not honor God, no matter how well we try to do it. At best we'll be imposters, emotionally deflated and physically exhausted from trying to live someone else's life. But when we consecrate and commit our gifts to Him in this current phase of life, we'll see that He will empower us to use them in a way that will not only yield honor and glory to Himself, but also bring us fulfilment and satisfaction. You can be confident that what you have to offer, when focused on honoring Him instead of impressing or imitating others, will bring your best to the forefront.

What *you* can do—yes, you!—is good enough.

Did you hear me?

Good.

This might be news to you, especially if your natural inclination is to wish you could do things like *her*, like *them*. Maybe then "God would get a little glory out of this life of mine." But Paul's instructions and this resolution are not meant to inspire you to become like somebody else—to start doing more of the things *they* do, more like *they* do them. It's calling for "whatever *you* do." There is value in the unique way that *you* mother your children, love your husband, do your job, oversee that committee, participate in that organization, and spend your time. It's what *you* do. It's how *you* do it. And that's what He has promised to undergird with His power, causing Himself to be magnified through your actions.

My late mother, Lois, had to come to this realization as a young pastor's wife. She got the idea (after some not-so-subtle suggestions) that she was supposed to fit a certain profile in her highly visible position. She was to play the piano, lead the choir, run the women's ministry, and dress with sophisticated style and taste. That's what others thought she should do. Yet much of this was not what God had equipped her or called her to do. She could not possibly engage herself actively in everyone's expectations and do any of them with much success. So instead of trying to do what other pastors' wives had done or were doing, or what people in the congregation were expecting of her, she decided to consider carefully what *she* had been gifted to do and how she could do those particular things with all her might, as unto the Lord.

Mom found her "whatever you do" spot—the one where you can actually experience the joy of doing "everything for God's glory."

So take a second to consider what God has uniquely equipped and given you a passion to do, as well as what He's asking of you (and what He's *not* asking of you) at this particular season of life. Instead of focusing on what you *can't* do, prayerfully consider how to capitalize on what you *can* do in a way that will tap into God's presence and power. Then no matter what day it is, no matter how old you are, no matter what the moment demands, you can be yourself, fully believing that your personal "whatever you do" is fulfilling the purposes of God and will bring Him honor.

In anything and everything.

And here's something else: the message of Paul's verse—"whether you eat or drink, or whatever you do"—suggests that we shouldn't wait until matters are more important before honoring God becomes our primary goal. Hardly anything could be more regular, mundane, and ritualistic than eating and drinking. But nothing in God's eyes is too menial to be considered worthy of our wholehearted devotion. Everything He has purposed for us to participate in—every little thing—is a fresh, available opportunity for His glory to be seen through us, through you. Therefore, the task set before you right now holds the potential for bringing honor to the Lord. That's why He's given it to you. Yes, the paperwork and details of your desk job. Yes, the editing and design of your social media posts. Yes, the changing of another dirty diaper. Yes, the small deed of kindness to your husband.

Don't save your best for later.

Don't wait to finish school, reserving your best work for whenever you land a real job that's actually taking you somewhere. Don't wait until you're married when the things you do will feel more like they're contributing to building a home and a life. Don't wait until you start a family, thinking you'll be more inspired to give your best when you have children to invest in. Don't wait until your kids leave the nest, biding your time until you're freer to pour yourself into the next challenge.

Scout out what God's Spirit is compelling you to do, and believe that if He called you to it, He will empower you to do it in a way that brings honor to Him. Then cooperate with Him. Bring your best to it right now. Right here. Right away.

I learned this lesson from my friend Tina. She never did anything halfway. When Tina did something, everybody knew it. If she agreed to help you out, you could be sure you'd get everything Tina had to give. Fully engaged. All over it. She didn't believe in halfhearted participation . . . in anything.

A single woman, Tina lived in an apartment. And though she longed to own a home, she relished her little living space and filled it full with her vibrant style and personality. Despite the fact that she was renting, she insisted on adding the small touches that made her temporary housing arrangement a home. She repainted the walls, upgraded the lighting fixtures, installed some new appliances. She gave that little place a soul.

I remember asking her one time why she was investing so much into a place that most people wouldn't sink a dime into. She told me that she never wanted to treat anything in her life as if it wasn't worth celebrating, as if it was too ordinary to deserve extraordinary attention and appreciation. She didn't want to wait until she was married or owned a house to start being a good steward of her home. She didn't want to put off creating a life for herself and the people she loved. She didn't want to shortchange the glory of God by limiting it to things that seemed suitably grand in scope. So she nested. Settled in. Right there in apartment 21A. Brought the best of herself to this less-than-ideal but better-than-nothing time and space.

Her words and attitude really hit home the day I filed by her casket with the other mourners, shocked to see her frail, lifeless body surrounded by white satin cushions, taken so soon and suddenly from our smiling embrace and friendship. She had gone to be with the Lord long before she or anyone else expected. But what if she had been the kind of woman who waited until her life was a little more together and established before she really started to live? What if she had held herself back and reserved her best for later?

Please don't wait for another time, another set of circumstances, another accomplishment, or another pay raise before flinging the full weight of your potential into the mix—even if you're not entirely happy with how your life looks right now.

Maybe you envisioned yourself running a Fortune 500 company rather than being a homemaker. And yet I wonder if some of those same skills you've honed and enjoyed using in other settings are exactly "the best" of you that God would have you bring to the job of being CEO of the day-to-day operations in your home.

Bring your best.

Maybe you have a serious passion for ministry and wish you were financially able to engage in it full-time rather than being saddled with shift work that pays the bills but keeps you tied down to a firm schedule and thirty-minute lunches. Don't wait until you're on the mission field to fuel that fire. I wonder if that zeal is exactly "the best" of you that God wants your coworkers and clients to encounter on the mission field that doubles as your corporate environment.

Bring your best.

Maybe divorce has left you alone and stripped of confidence, a shell of the woman you once carried into church, school functions, and family gatherings. But what if you knew God's glory was still imbedded in you—in *this* piece and *that* piece—and by putting all of yourself into all that's still here, you could once again experience the pleasure of honoring Him by every little thing you do?

Bring your best—all your gifts, skills, talents, and abilities to the task at hand—in this moment, for His glory.

Without a martyr complex.

Even if no one notices.

Even if they notice but don't appreciate your efforts.

Do it anyway. For His glory.

In anything, everything, and whatever you do.

- *Carefully consider this sentence in light of your own personal circumstances, then record your specific thoughts about it: "When honoring God is your one thing, it pares down your purpose and narrows your focus."*

- *How does a focus on honoring God . . .*
     a. lighten the burden of the perfectionist?
     b. inspire you to give your best effort?

- *In which tasks have you felt like your best efforts were not good enough?*

- *When faced with an activity like this—one that you find particularly challenging—how are you encouraged by knowing that God will empower your efforts designed to bring Him glory?*

It Only Works When I Breathe

My family and I have become professional travelers. We've learned how to pack lightly and navigate an airport in no time flat. We've pretty much gotten it down to a science. From an early age, my boys became so familiar with planes and airports, they started to mimic the airline attendants and their preflight spiels. You know . . .

- "Please keep your seat belt fastened while the 'Fasten Seat Belt' sign is lit."
- "Lock your tray tables and bring your seat backs to an upright position."
- "If you're seated in an emergency exit row but do not wish to perform the functions described in the event of an emergency, please ask a flight attendant to reseat you."

But no instruction was more entertaining to my young sons than when the attendant stood up to do his or her little demonstration, pulled out a clear plastic bag attached to a yellow cone with two little strings hanging down from it, and said, "In case of an emergency, oxygen masks will automatically drop down and appear in front of you. If you are traveling with a child—(or anyone *acting* like a child, as one stewardess added)—secure your own mask first, and then assist the other person."

This one always bothered my boys. "Why should the adult get the mask first?" they wondered. It seemed natural to them that the kids should go first. (So typical.)

I did my best to explain that children can't receive proper aid until the person helping them is capable of doing so. If I were to pass out from lack of oxygen, for example, I wouldn't be able to provide them the care they needed and deserved.

Such is life. You can't care for others if you yourself are uncared for.

Are you suffocating while trying to make sure everyone else is stable? That's the question I want you to consider before you sign the next resolution.

Over the last three chapters I've encouraged you to give the best of yourself to others, and yet doing so will be impossible if you don't have anything to give. A fatigued, unhealthy body will not have the energy to make it through the day. Skills and mental capabilities that have been dulled and left unattended will not have the sharpness required to be of full use to your calling and divine mission. Not being spiritually attuned to the Lord and His Word will cause you to be deflated, lacking the Spirit's direction and the fruit He wants to yield through your life.

Therefore, making time to "secure your mask" is not a luxury; it's a *necessity* for any woman wanting to make this resolution. You will never be able to give the best of yourself if you're not taking care of yourself to begin with.

I'm well aware of the difficulty I may have presented here. Having the time to do anything for yourself may seem out of the question— maybe even highly selfish, given your time constraints as a single mother of two small children, or a mom with a special-needs child, or a grown daughter with aging parents, or a wife whose husband's career keeps him on the road several days a week, or a single professional saddled with a tall stack of obligations. This list could go on, couldn't it? And whichever phrase would best describe you, it would probably mitigate against the ready availability of any personal time for yourself.

At the beginning of this section, when I asked you to rearrange your boxes, I'm almost certain that many of the ones pertaining to the things that are fulfilling to you personally were the ones you reassigned to the back of the line. That's usually where our own care goes when we start getting serious about life. Many women assume and are taught that these are the sacrifices we should make to squeeze the most from each minute in the day and maximize our time. So we feel terribly guilty when we even *consider* taking a moment to renew and rejuvenate.

But hold on a minute. Why wouldn't taking care of yourself be considered one of the best possible uses of your time when doing so sets the tone for the rest of your entire life?

Now I know that not everyone can head off to the spa for half-day treatments once a week or do shopping and lunch with their girlfriends every afternoon. Certainly not me. Time and money keep these luxuries from being feasible for most of us. Neither am I giving you a license to be self-absorbed.

I *am* saying this, however: *if you don't have any oxygen, you will begin to suffocate*. That's just the truth, my "I can do everything, don't worry about me, I'll be fine, thank you" friend.

So . . .

What simple pleasure could you participate in that would rejuvenate you? Many of us don't even know what simple fun looks like anymore.

For me, spending a few moments alone doing the grocery shopping, or sneaking off to a movie with a friend once a month constitutes good self-care. Putting on a pair of sneakers and heading out the front door for an hour-long walk while listening to my worship-song playlist always refreshes me. And sometimes, when those afternoon hours bring a lull that woos me to sleep, a quick thirty-minute nap recalibrates my energy level.

It's also been recommended to me, as I've gotten older, that I mustn't be afraid to consider the changing needs of my body and restructure my life to facilitate those needs. What my body required to stay replenished, energized, and healthy ten years ago is different from what it needs today. This has meant reconsidering what foods I eat, what vitamins I take, and the consistency with which I see health-care professionals throughout the year. Additionally, I try not to allow the passions God has given me to get trampled under the busyness of life. This is hard to do and requires intentionality. So, as I'm able, I incorporate small activities and interests that help me continue to cultivate, develop, and stay in tune with those areas.

What might give *you* a fresh draft of oxygen? It doesn't have to be expensive or particularly time-consuming. A walk after dinner. A cup of tea at a friend's kitchen table. Picking up that novel that's been sitting on your nightstand. Getting to the office ten minutes early to be alone with God before the workday starts. Often a quick interval of quiet (for an introvert) or social engagement (for an extrovert) can give you just the boost you need to be back on your feet and ready for the tasks at hand.

Set a timer if you have to. But *do it*!

There's just no way around it. If you're going to stay sharp—if you're going to keep your oxygen levels up—you need a break every now and then. It's not a break *from* your life; it's a break *for* your life.

If you live with someone—your husband, a roommate—ask him or her to help ensure that this becomes a regular part of your life. If this kind of household accountability is not an option for you, consider if there are people within your own church who could help you with this. For instance, there are other moms around with the same time constraints you have. What if you arranged to keep one another's children for two-hour intervals on occasion so that one of you could have a few minutes to run errands alone?

Or what if there's a single woman who really wants to know what it's like to be a wife and mother? In exchange for your real-life mentorship, maybe she could come over to get some hands-on experience for an hour here or there and give you enough time to do something that would really recharge you or give you a sense of accomplishment.

Or maybe if you live close to a friend, the two of you could arrange a little cooking co-op. If you're already preparing a meal one night, why not make enough for both of your families so the other mom can make use of the time when she'd normally be fixing dinner? Then take turns so that both of you can benefit from the trade-off. Creatively consider how you could arrange small pockets of time like this so you can snatch some moments for yourself.

And single woman, I want to warn you against assuming—just because you're single—that you're off the hook on this topic. Some of the busiest, most overwhelmed people I know are single. Without the built-in personal restraints a married woman might have, it can become easy to overextend yourself. You're going to bed late and waking up even earlier the next day. You're busier than any one person should be, showing up at a lot of activities but often unable to offer your best because you're so tired all the time, losing your grip on your primary callings. More critically, if you choose to be married later in life, you're setting a precedent that will follow you into this new season. Engaging in good self-care now will help you develop a habit that continues to benefit you throughout your life.

I've often heard that the best gift a couple can give their children is a healthy marriage. And yet with the daily demands of parenting, one of the hardest things to do is to spend time with your husband, building your friendship, enjoying your partnership, keeping the passion alive. The same is true for you as a woman. The best gift you can give those you love is to take care of yourself, even though it can be one of the hardest things for you to prioritize.

And yet by running yourself ragged, trying to do everything morning till night, you're in essence trying to be God. But listen to me carefully. Overwork is a form of unbelief. You're saying through your actions that you don't believe He can take care of everything, meaning *you're* on the hook for it. But playing God is exhausting. After all, He's the only One up to the job.

So take a step back from your life, take a fresh look at it, and ask yourself:

"When will I put on my oxygen mask so I can . . . bre-e-e-eathe?"

- *By signing this resolution, you are choosing not to allow perfectionism to rule your life. You are determining, rather, to consider carefully what God has prioritized for you in this season of life, and then examine the unique qualities you've been given to bring to those tasks. You are accepting this resolution as an invitation to become fully engaged in today's assignment and bring all of yourself into every one. You will no longer see taking care of yourself as something to be ashamed of but a requirement to enable you to better serve others. Consider your notes from the pervious chapters, and then make your resolution with confidence.*

❧ MY BEST ☙

I will seek to devote the best of myself, my time, and my talents to the primary roles the Lord has entrusted to me in this phase of my life.

_____

MY BLESSING

*A resolution to esteem others with my time,
concern, and full attention*

The Gift

Love is patient. (1 Corinthians 13:4)

On the heels of receiving my undergraduate degree, I began working as an independent contract speaker for the Zig Ziglar Corporation. At the time, I had no idea I would end up in full-time ministry or just how much speaking and teaching this path would include. These formative years proved an invaluable training ground filled with unique opportunities to sit under the tutelage of some amazing presenters, including Mr. Ziglar. I was the young one of the bunch, so I took great care when watching these much more seasoned communicators, studying what they did with their hands, how they made effective use of the stage, how they engaged an audience, everything.

I especially recall listening to one of the eldest and most accomplished speakers on our team deliver a message I'd heard him share a million times before. I could probably have told you every word he was going to say before he said it. Yet at the end of his talk, something he mentioned affected me in a way it had never touched me before. Right before taking his seat after an hour-long presentation, he lowered his voice, looked squarely into the eyes of his audience, and said, "I'm aware that the greatest gift you can ever give someone is the gift of your own time. Thank you for giving me that gift today."

Time. Listening.

A gift.

I've never forgotten that. In fact, I keep this awareness at the forefront of my mind each time I stand on a platform in front of a listening
audience. When people give you their ear, they are offering you a sliver
of their life they can never retrieve again—one of the few gifts that can
never be returned or retracted.

But this dynamic is not only true of an audience listening to a
speaker. It's true of any person who lends her ear to another individual
in personal conversation and interaction. We are in that position every
day—the opportunity to envelop ourselves in someone else's words, to
suppress the clamor of our own thoughts and schedule, to focus our
full attention on other people, and to express love to them by being
patient with them, giving them an offering of the rarest kind. The gift of
ourselves. The gift of our time.

The gift of listening.

Think of it. When was the last time somebody really listened to
you? Not the last time you talked but the last time you felt you were
really heard. It's highly probable that these two occasions were not
one and the same. You may not even be able to easily recall a recent
moment when you experienced that special sense of knowing that
someone was all there, all yours, intent on hearing what you had to
say and not rushing you to hurry up and finish. But once you trans-
port yourself back to that time, seeing the attentive eyes of that other
person, you'll be looking into the face of someone you deeply appreciate, someone who truly knows how to make a person feel valued and
accepted, loved and affirmed.

This is what the gift of listening does. It mushrooms into others—
the gifts of self-worth, significance, personal satisfaction. The kind of
gifts we all want to be known for giving.

But, oh, how uncommon they are. How rarely we receive them,
much less give them. Most of the time we're so focused on ourselves
and preoccupied with our own feelings, every conversation becomes
ultimately about us and how we're being affected. We're parsing what
the other person is saying, interpreting as we go, trying to fix whatever

problem she's presenting, jumping in at every possible opening with our own attempts to turn the attention back to us, our experiences, and our opinions. Even if we have good intentions, even when we try really hard to make ourselves listen, we have a tough time keeping it up for long. And every time our focus lags, we translate to the other person a disinterest not only in what she's talking about but in herself as a person.

Truly, what we say by *not* listening says a lot.

Which is precisely why this simple yet profoundly difficult discipline is such a source of extreme blessing to others. When someone is able to know, during whatever few moments we're present with her, that we esteem and honor who she is—few things mean as much.

Don't the people in your life deserve this blessing? Your husband? Your children? Your parents? Your friends? To feel strengthened and encouraged just by being around you? Even without being able to give them money, or an ideal solution to their questions, or a job offer to ease their worry and desperation, you can still cause them to sense a gentle strength and empowerment in your presence. Whether friends or family members or even strangers—people you could just as easily pass by in your hurry to get from place to place—looking them in the eye can be a blessing you share throughout the day. Every day.

Jesus must have known the power of this blessing. He made a habit of bestowing it on the most insignificant, unnoticed people of His day. Jesus—the only true know-it-all ever to walk the earth, who legitimately had no good reason for listening to a single word from anyone—chose on many occasions to stop, to wait, to listen, to give attention to another before speaking Himself, even when the other person was misinformed or spouting blasphemy.

He listened to the clever dodges and smokescreens of the woman at the well (John 4:4–30). He listened to Peter and the other disciples indignantly boasting that they would never deny or desert Him (Matthew 26:31–35). He listened to the call of an individual blind man, even over the mournful roar of human need on a crowded street near Jericho (Luke 18:35–43).

We should hardly be surprised. This is so consistent with His character. Even throughout the Old Testament we see Yahweh listening to His people. Listening to the accusatory sentiments of a discouraged, impatient prophet (Habakkuk 1:1–11). Listening to the delineated questions of a man suffering unexplained misery (Job 3:1–26). Listening to the many excuses mapped out by Moses for why he was uniquely unqualified for locking horns with Pharaoh (Exodus 3:1–4:13). Listening to the whining tirade of a bitter, unbecoming man of God (Jonah 4:1–11).

Listening is one of the most significant ways He blesses us. Therefore, quite predictably, it's one of the key ways we can bless others.

So choose to listen. Resist the urge to criticize, insult, laugh, prematurely interject, or make sarcastic remarks. Battle the press of time and urgency and the hunger to get away. Just lean in, quietly, emphatically, purposefully.

And listen.

It's your gift. Your blessing.

Give it to whomever you can.

• *What is the most difficult part of listening for you?*

• *Recall the last time you genuinely felt heard. Make a list of some one-word adjectives that describe how this encounter made you feel about what you were saying? About yourself?*

• *Who are the people in your life who would benefit the most if you took the time to listen to them?*

Shhhh

One month before my wedding day in 1999, I came across a little book on marriage that contained an insightful definition of *wisdom*: (1) knowing what to say, and (2) not saying it.

Of all the things I'd read and heard through various newlywed books and bits of premarital advice, something about this simple statement seemed to leap off the page and linger in the air, challenging me, convicting me, redirecting me. Even today—even right this minute—I'm captured by both its brevity and perspicacity.

It still speaks to me. Telling me that wisdom is often revealed in silence.

Granted, this wasn't entirely new information. My own mother said something similar to me—or at least to the much mouthier version of me who shared this same body during my teenage years and often spoke without thinking. "Priscilla," she said, "you don't have to say everything that pops into your head." But my mom, of course, wasn't the first to communicate this sage advice. Long before I was a teenager, certainly long before I was on the precipice of becoming a wife, a man of great wisdom chronicled the following words into Scripture:

Too much talk leads to sin. Be sensible and keep
your mouth shut. (Proverbs 10:19 NLT)

So I'd had ample opportunity for this idea to grip me. I knew of the beauty, power, and (yes) wisdom involved in carefully considering what I say and when I choose to say it. I was fully aware that the strongest, most astonishing stance of all is often silence.

But I haven't always lived like it.

I distinctly remember a time when Jerry and I were picked up by an older, silver-haired gentleman and his wife at the airport in Los Angeles, where I'd gone to minister at a local conference. On the way to our accommodations at a tiny parish house across from the church, we began a conversation about spiritual things. When the man mentioned a specific passage in keeping with the theme of our discussion, it happened to be one I'd just been reading on the flight over. So when he specifically said where the verse was found, I knew immediately that he was incorrect.

"I think that's in 1 Corinthians 3," I corrected him.

"Nope," the kind, soft-spoken man replied confidently to me through the rearview mirror, "It's definitely 2 Corinthians 4."

Quietly I flipped through my Bible and found the passage tucked exactly where I knew it was. Then without thinking I lifted it up in view of his gaze in the mirror, pointing out that he was clearly wrong. "It's 1 Corinthians 3."

I win.

Here I was, barely in my mid-twenties, choosing to take on a man in his seventies who'd been kind enough to invite a kid like me to California—*over a disputed Scripture reference!* Instead of just staying quiet and allowing this sweet man to maintain his dignity, I'd spoken up, pretty much spoiling the mood of the rest of our ride together.

When Jerry and I were finally alone, he asked me, "Why did you do that? Why was it so important to know you were right?" I don't know. I just know there's not a single one of us who doesn't have a personal story or two (or twenty) like this—a time when being quiet would have spared us all kinds of hurt, embarrassment, and regret—when our silence might have prevented us from landing a damaging blow to another or straining a relationship.

Silence is our friend. Silence is our strength.

Obviously I'm not saying we should never speak up or should change our core personalities. Using our voice is one of our most potent gifts. It's just that we probably don't need any instructions in this book on how to be better talkers. Let's be honest, we've pretty much got the talking part mastered, don't we? But a chapter on understanding the wisdom and power of silence—the last thing we often consider when faced with a situation we feel is begging for our opinion, or an infuriating comment on Twitter that seems to demand our response, or an awkward stillness yawning to be filled in—that's something worth reminding ourselves about.

Silence is our way of growing deep, of discovering maturity, of exercising the kind of restraint and influence God has created us to have on others, as opposed to the destructive, discouraging alternative. "Knowing what to say" and "not saying it" at an inappropriate time puts us in a position where—when the time is right for expressing ourselves—our words can yield an extremely positive blessing.

A woman who is quick to listen is one who gathers up all the information before releasing her reaction in personal conversation or a public forum. She resists the urge to spout off everything her mind formulates, choosing rather to give her solutions time to settle, to become properly shaped before being shared. When she speaks, her advice and assessments are sensible and sober. Prudent and purposeful. Not knee-jerk reactions to other people's foolish comments. Those on the receiving end of her conversation realize they're hearing a response that hasn't been considered halfheartedly. They're primed to listen on the edge of their seats—eager, hungry, ready to hear—knowing that "the tongue of the righteous is pure silver" (Proverbs 10:20). Valuable, prized, precious, and worthy. Words that nourish, edify, and benefit others.

I know you've met these exceptional kinds of people. Women of uncommon wisdom and dignity. You've wanted, as I have, to be the kind of person who sits at the end of the dinner table fully present by your quiet strength and peaceful wisdom, by your patience and prudence. Rather than being tangled up in a web of pointless gossip—some "he said, she said" mayhem that's not intended to be solved but merely enjoyed for sport—you hold your opinions, knowing that the incessant chatter of "foolish lips will be destroyed" (Proverbs 10:8).

Yes, picture yourself as that person. Someone who's long abandoned the need to impress others or be the center of attention. In its place you've acquired the ease and freedom that unsaddles you from pride and pretense, from anything that compels you to desire being noticed or to force your importance onto the group. In humility and appreciation of others, you're content just being a participant like everyone else, contributing as much by what you let others say as by what you add to the conversation yourself. You don't think you're always right and that everyone else is wrong, as if you alone know all the answers. You just listen and learn. Contemplating and considering. Weighing and waiting.

This is wisdom.

And power.

It's the power of the tongue, as described by James in the New Testament. The sure, steady strength of character available to the person who's able to harness it, bridle it, and contain its wild nature. "For we all stumble in many ways," he tells us, but "if anyone does not stumble in what he says, he is mature, able also to control the whole body" (James 3:2). Gaining mastery over our words is like a sea captain caught in a furious squall over open waters who strategically applies the small rudder underneath his massive oceangoing vessel, charting its course and ultimately determining its destination, bringing it safely to shore.

The blessing of silence. May we learn it, love it, and live according to it.

This is our resolution.

- *What would immediately change for the better in your life if you began exercising the spiritual restraint of silence?*

- *Try it for just a day or two. Deliberately keep from saying something that's better left unsaid. Allow the bait of another's unkind or inappropriate remark to land without hooking a response from you. Record what you observe about yourself and the change in the dynamics around you.*

Underneath It All

My sister Chrystal and I shared a room growing up. It was a small twelve-by-thirteen-foot space with our twin-sized beds lining opposite walls. Mine was right next to the Jack and Jill bathroom that connected to our brothers' room. At night we'd close that door before going to sleep to keep from being distracted by them. (You know brothers.)

I distinctly remember waking up one morning and looking above the frame of that bathroom door—the same sight I was accustomed to seeing every morning at sunrise. But this time I noticed something I didn't remember ever being there before: a slight, slender crack creeping upward about two feet from the top of the door to the ceiling.

Strange.

When my dad found out about it, he called a painter to come over and look at it. I remember him showing up a few days later, applying some plaster and repainting with the most compatible color he could find. For several weeks after that, I went to bed looking at the misplaced line of color streaked on the wall above the door.

Then one day I awoke startled to see that the crack had returned. And this time he wasn't alone. He apparently had been recommending his new living arrangements to his family members because it appeared they'd all come to settle in with him. As many as a half-dozen cracks of all shapes and sizes now laced the wall.

But when another painter came to examine the situation, he told my dad that painting alone wouldn't be sufficient to solve the problem. The reason the cracks were showing up, he explained, was because the foundation underneath our house was shifting. And no matter how much paint we splashed up there to cover them, they would keep coming back. The cracks were merely symptoms of a more serious condition.

The only way to rectify this problem was to address the foundation.

All of this talk about being a blessing to others by disciplining ourselves to listen and by preparing thoughtful, careful responses has gotten me thinking about how difficult a resolution this will be for many of us. I could probably venture to say . . . *most* of us.

Or even more accurately . . . *me.*

Controlling my own tongue is a quest that I'm sure will require all the maturity every year of my life will bring. That's because so far along this journey, I've already discovered that the "cracks" I make with my mouth are actually symptoms of a much deeper, much more intimate issue, something much more difficult to address. It's down below the surface. Closer to the ground than my mouth is.

> *For out of the abundance (overflow) of the heart*
> *his mouth speaks. (Luke 6:45 AMP)*

Turns out, my mouth is only a barometer that divulges whether I'm immersed in humility and surrendered in obedience to the Lord, or I'm housing a malnourished spirit that stubbornly refuses to yield to the wisdom of God's own Word.

It's a foundational issue.

So taking inventory of your tongue's track record is an instructive way to uncover what's hidden within. Let's try it.

• *Symptom:* Are you always quick to offer an opinion, inserting your assessments into conversations at every conceivable opportunity? *Diagnosis:* This could reveal a haughty tinge in your heart, which causes you to feel the need to impress and be at the center of attention.

• *Symptom:* Are you constantly critical and demeaning in your spoken sentiments? *Diagnosis:* These are often code words for insecurity and a lack of certainty in your inherent value, as well as a heart infested with anger and judgmental attitudes.

• *Symptom:* Do you frequently find yourself instigating arguments or being divisive among others? *Diagnosis:* You're lacking a spirit of peace and unity deep inside, a true desire for your relationships to be strengthened and reflect the grace of Christ.

• *Symptom:* Does gossip continue to come easily for you, drawing you into unsavory and unhelpful exchanges? *Diagnosis:* You find others' problems and difficulties entertaining and don't think of them as humans needing your support, prayer, and companionship.

• *Symptom:* Do your words often reveal a doubtful, skeptical outlook? *Diagnosis:* You're low in the faith and belief department, not operating from a deep trust in God's ability and His wise handling of the details and timing of your life.

The words of our lips are like cracks in the wall, revealing what's going on at the foundation. For truly, "out of the abundance (overflow) of the heart his mouth speaks."

Jesus' use of the word *heart* in this verse signifies the inner being of an individual, the place where our thoughts, attitudes, and beliefs are cemented. The heart is a reservoir, a holding tank for every attitude and belief we've either placed there or allowed to hang out there. It is a storehouse containing the essence of who we are and—because of its direct link to our ongoing habits and actions—the picture of who we're becoming.

And just as surging floodwaters will burst through a dam, just as sizzling popcorn kernels will erupt on the cooking stove, the contents of our hearts will inevitably push and press against the sides, unable to stay contained, needing more room to expand, and eventually spilling out in our words and conversation. Can't help it. No stopping it.

When I'm in the car with my youngest son, Jude, for example, he immediately spots every single Chik-fil-A we pass, and he always makes a point of letting me know he sees it. Even when that trademark red logo is still quite a distance away, my boy seems to have some sort of radar that clues him in to an approaching fast-food opportunity. Why? *Because that's what he loves.*

And what goes for chicken tenders and salty waffle fries goes for anything else we set our hearts on. Those hidden loves, desires, and tendencies blow their cover in our conversations.

The Bible refers to these occupants of our hearts as "treasure."

> *The good man out of the good treasure of his heart*
> *brings forth what is good; and the evil man out of the evil*
> *treasure brings forth what is evil. (Luke 6:45 NASB)*

This word for "treasure" in the original language is the same one used to describe what was inside the chest the wise men in Matthew 2 carried. The reason they were able to pull such fine gifts *out of it* to present to Jesus was because those were the treasures they had placed *in it.* Likewise, the kinds of treasure—whether good or bad—that flow from our hearts into our conversations, our reactions, our initiatives, and our expressions will determine whether we come bearing harm or blessing.

So I ask you . . .

What are you putting inside?

What treasures are you storing?

If you don't know, just listen to yourself, because your words and tone and topics of conversation will tell you. This is why it's so imperative that you heed this remarkable piece of biblical advice:

> *Watch over your heart with all diligence, for from it flow*
> *the springs of life. (Proverbs 4:23 NASB)*

You must be the guardian of your own heart, ensuring that you do not allow it to become polluted by anything that will hinder your mission of being conformed into the likeness of Christ. The more you soak in His Word and His truth, the more you can expect to have a deep reservoir filled with all the treasures needed to temper your conversations with wisdom, kindness, and humility.

So guard your heart, and do not allow it to become hardened (Proverbs 28:14), deceptive (Psalm 12:2), prideful (Proverbs 21:4), or unclean (Psalm 51:10). Seek rather to have a heart that is always sensitive to the prodding of God's Spirit (Romans 8:5), single-mindedly devoted to Him (Psalm 86:11), drenched in humility (Proverbs 22:4), and pure before God (Matthew 5:8). "Do nothing out of selfish ambition or conceit, but in humility consider others as more important than yourselves. Everyone should look not to his own interests, but rather to the interests of others" (Philippians 2:3–4).

A woman whose heart is full of gratitude and humility, who is certain of God's love for her, and who genuinely prizes the worth of those around her will release a steady stream of graciousness that will refresh others through her conversation. Others will desire the joy of her company because they know she seeks their welfare and esteems them highly. She will invite the opportunity to listen to others, then will humbly offer the wisdom that is rooted in her treasure box, filled with a wealth of good things.

So before you prayerfully consider and sign the next resolution, please understand that it's not just about watching your mouth but watching your heart. Any lasting change you make in controlling your speech will have to start at the base, the foundation, down where the cracks are really formed.

Down where breakthroughs can really happen.

- *As you prepare to make this resolution, picture the people in your life who most need to receive this gift from you, as well as the obstacles that often keep you from being able to give it. Before rushing ahead and signing your name, consider what changes you'll need to make to become a person who is "quick to listen and slow to speak." Do you need to turn off some technological devices, for example, so people feel prioritized and important? Be willing to make some of these practical and necessary adjustments so this resolution doesn't just "sit*

on the shelf" of your life and not become a reality. Then, when you're ready, prayerfully read the statement below and sign your name.

❧ MY BLESSING ❧

I will be a woman who is quick to listen and slow to speak. I will care about the concerns of others and esteem them more highly than myself.

_____

MY FORGIVENESS

*A resolution to release others from the prison
of my hurt and anger*

Internal Injuries

ER, a classic medical drama series, ran on television from 1994–2009, inviting the audience into the frenetic and heart-rending world of the emergency room at Chicago's County General Hospital. Maybe you enjoyed it like I did. One night (before on-demand viewing was a thing), I curled up on the sofa right on time to watch the latest episode. I didn't want to miss the beginning since those first moments were always packed with a riveting scene that would set the stage for the rest of the story line. This one didn't disappoint.

A devastating crash brought dozens of wounded to the emergency room, overwhelming the staff with the sheer number of those needing attention. Among the flurry of new patients were two women—best friends—who had both been involved in the accident.

One of the women appeared to be fine. But the other, strapped to a gurney, was obviously in grave danger. The attendants rushed to her aid, whisking her into triage, while several nurses offered the less injured woman a quick check of her vitals, just to be sure she was okay. Far more concerned about the health of her closest friend, she declined.

As the program continued, chronicling the various stories and traumas surrounding this event, the camera kept circling back to this frantically worried woman. She prayed by her friend's bedside. She hailed the doctors' and nurses' attention, requesting pain medication and assistance for her ailing companion. She made cell phone calls to family members. She kept up a one-sided conversation with her semi-conscious friend in an unselfish attempt to keep her company. Finally, when the stricken woman's condition appeared to be stabilizing, her relieved friend relaxed a bit and began to entertain the medical staff with her effervescent, engaging personality and wit. Everything seemed to be turning out all right. Not only was her friend going to be fine; so was she.

Then all of a sudden, with absolutely no warning, she collapsed.

Just like that.

I sat forward in my seat, stunned, just like the fictional hospital staff. Highly trained individuals, who seconds before had been laughing at her jokes while caring for her injured friend, now gathered around this woman, quickly administering the help she so desperately needed.

But nothing they could do was of any value.

Within sixty seconds she was dead.

Gone.

A CT scan revealed that she had apparently suffered internal wounds and bleeding in the accident. And throughout the day—though neither she nor any of the hospital staff had been aware of it—her life had been slowly ebbing away. Internal bleeding. For hours on end, she had been within an arm's length of treatment and healing procedures, while secretly dying on the inside. She had cared for another person without realizing the extent of her own injuries, without recognizing she was fighting for her own life as well.

Such is the trauma of unforgiveness—the worst internal injury of all. It can easily go undetected, masked beneath the disguises of external smiles and laughter. We pour ourselves into activity and busyness to avoid having to think about it, medicating ourselves on others' needs instead of tending to the surgery we need ourselves. We continually operate at surface level, masters at managing the externals, even though the churn of sickness and unrest is always at work underneath, wreaking havoc and decay to our very souls.

"Examine yourselves," the apostle Paul declared—not just once but twice in the span of two books of the Bible (1 Corinthians 11:28; 2 Corinthians 13:5). Rather than always spending your time trying to fix others, look deeply and consider what could be festering inside your own heart—what the Bible calls a "root of bitterness" (Hebrews 12:15), growing in the soil of your heart and sprouting buds of resentment that affect every aspect of your life.

We're embarking in the following pages on a journey into forgiveness. Maybe this is not an area of concern for you right now, so you're tempted to skip to the next section. But I encourage you to hang in there with me because this resolution will most likely be beneficial to your life at some point in the future. However, if this theme settles squarely on a specific pain in your heart, then prepare yourself for what could be one of the most difficult yet worthwhile ventures of your whole life.

Obviously the span of a few thousand words is hardly adequate even to *approach* the subject, much less wrap our full arms around it. But for a few moments at least, let's take a look inward, you and me. Instead of working so hard to keep the focus and spotlight on everyone else—both those who've hurt us as well as those who make us feel better and forget about it all—let's be willing to drag out these grudges we're holding and harboring, these heavy containers of unforgiveness that never stop leaching poisons into our system.

Let's "examine" ourselves. Because if we do, we could be on our way to healing.

We could live.

Really live.

- *If you don't feel like forgiveness is something you have an issue with, list some practical ways you can continue to see to it "that no root of bitterness springs up, causing trouble" (Hebrews 12:15).*

• *Are you more prone to care for others than to examine and tend to your own spiritual needs? If so, how does this manifest itself in your life?*

• *Prayerfully consider: Who, if anyone, are the people you harbor unforgiveness toward? How have you seen this affect your life?*

• *Grab your Bible and choose one passage to read and study on forgiveness:*

  • Mark 11:25–26—making reconciled relationships a regular part of our praying
  • Matthew 6:14–15—how our forgiveness of others relates to God's forgiveness of us
  • Hebrews 12:14—the blessing that flows from pursuing peace with everyone

• *On bitterness:*

  • Ephesians 4:31—the only good thing to do with it is to get rid of it
  • Hebrews 12:15—what bitterness can do if it's not pulled up by the roots
  • Proverbs 14:10—all we can ever expect from hanging on to it

All Clear

Book covers fascinate me. Strategically done, great covers tell their own story and captivate potential readers before they've read even a single word inside. The challenge to those who design them comes from attempting to create a single piece of imagery—whether it involves photography, color, texture, or whatever—that instantly delivers the message or mood of the book at a single glance. You see it, you get it, you want it.

You know *exactly* the experience that book is offering you.

One of my favorite covers of all time is from a book titled *Choosing Forgiveness*, written by my friend Nancy DeMoss Wolgemuth. The design is simple yet expressive. Directly above the title is a portion of a computer keyboard—just a small grouping of common keys. You can make out the blurred images of commands on each one. Right in the middle, however, highlighted a bit more than the rest, is one particular key. Clear, bold, and vibrant. A very specific button.

The delete button.

Because that's precisely what "choosing forgiveness" requires. It's a lot like pressing the delete key on our computers, backspacing over the accidents and unacceptable actions that have been written on the pages of our lives. Forgiveness means making the decision to move forward and create our next chapters while learning from but not being forced to incorporate the spoiled residue of the last ones. Pressing the delete key is a choice—a conclusive, one-time decision followed by an ongoing series of smaller yet equally important daily decisions to *continue* deleting, releasing the desire to hang on to what was done.

Even right this moment, as I sit here writing to you with my laptop centered on my legs, my fingers tapping the raised keys in front of me, how grateful I am for this little delete button just a short stretch away from my right pinky. If I happen to make a mistake (which is all too often the case) but I ignore the need to delete it, the remainder of that paragraph will be tied to the slipup. The entirety of my work will be marred by the glaring error I've left in place. By not completing the deliberate task of clearing it from the screen, I won't really be able to express what I'd meant my words to say. Not deleting it allows an incorrect occurrence to keep hanging around and causing trouble.

So I urge you to just pocket this little analogy.

The delete key.

You know what I'm talking about. Forgiving it. Ending it. No longer seeking vengeance or repayment.

And you know it's the right thing to do, even if it's the last thing you feel like doing.

But as hard as it can be to erase the harm that someone else has incorrectly typed into your life, some of the most difficult deleting you'll ever be called on to make is clearing the record of wrongs you've inflicted on yourself. Even if you can legitimately forgive others, you can't always seem to forgive yourself.

Years ago I had the opportunity to minister to a gathering of college-age women at a conference hosted by The Impact Movement, a ministry designed to reach out to African-American students on university campuses. During a girls-only session, I opened up the floor for questions and told the young women to feel free to ask anything they'd like. A shy young woman, her head hung down in personal disgust, stood from her seat and asked a question as simple as it was powerful: "How do you forgive yourself?"

All the other girls in the room turned their gaze from her to me, leaning in and listening intently, totally relating to where her question was coming from, and dying for someone to give them an answer.

Are you dying for somebody to give you one too?

Maybe you chose an abortion years ago. Maybe you caused an accident. Maybe you stirred up some unintentional chaos. Maybe you missed an opportunity that has cost you more money, heartache, and regret than you even want to think about. Maybe you've done any number of things that have made living harmoniously with yourself a nearly impossible task. You're reminded of it all the time. And you can't seem to forgive yourself, just as this girl couldn't. Her past mistakes were almost visibly swathed around her shoulders, bearing down with the force of dead weight only a past mistake can pack.

I answered her by telling her the same thing I want to share with you: *the capacity to forgive yourself is personally impossible.* You can't do it. Nobody can. But there's no need to be dismayed or defeated over this reality because absolutely no place in Scripture are we told that this is something we're supposed to do.

Hear that again: *the Bible doesn't tell us to forgive ourselves.*

Stick with me. I understand that guilt is an emotion that can crop up out of nowhere. Pushing the feeling aside, after repenting of the actions or inactions that first put it there, requires a deliberate, cognizant, daily act of faith. You must intentionally and consistently declare your heart and mind restored and refreshed even when you feel such deep regret. But you have no responsibility—or even *capability*, for that matter—to forgive yourself.

Here's the reality that you and I are instructed to rest in . . .

Everyone has sinned; we all fall short of God's glorious standard. Yet God, with undeserved kindness, declares that we are righteous. He did this through Christ Jesus when he freed us from the penalty for our sins. For God presented Jesus as the sacrifice for sin. People are made right with God when they believe that Jesus sacrificed his life, shedding his blood. This sacrifice shows that God was being fair when he held back and did not punish those who sinned in times past, for he was looking ahead and including them in what he would do in this present time. God did this to demonstrate his righteousness, for he himself is fair and just, and he declares sinners to be right in his sight when they believe in Jesus. (Romans 3:23–26 NLT)

Bottom line: forgiveness of your sins is something that Christ suffered a terrifying death to give you. And His work was so complete, He is thereby able to promise and declare to you and me, "I will forgive their iniquity and never again remember their sin" (Jeremiah 31:34). He has pressed the delete key over every sin you've ever committed. And He Himself—your ultimate ruler and judge—chooses never to recall your misdeeds to mind again, not with the intent of punishing you for them.

So why should *you*?

Actually, when you think about it, to say, "I can't forgive myself" means you don't fully believe that what He did was quite enough, that in some strange way His forgiveness of you is inadequate. This is the arrogant, hubristic tendency of fallen humanity, refusing to accept that His gift was and still is enough.

But, yes, it is.

And, yes, it must be. For no human forgiveness is strong enough— not even your own—to ever free you from the torturous reminder of your offense and the cloak of guilt it lays on your shoulders. Even if you were somehow able to find it and apply it, it wouldn't be enough. Only through a gracious acceptance of the gift extended to you through Christ Jesus will you ever really be free—free from the bondage, free from its hold, free to see that your Savior Himself pressed the delete button for your sins when He . . .

Walked the road to Calvary.

Felt the crown of thorns pressed onto His head.

Took the beating.

Allowed the sword's piercing.

Flinched against the nails puncturing His hands and feet.

Hung on Golgotha's tree.

That's when you received all the forgiveness you'll ever need. When He cried, "It is finished!" (John 19:30), it was done. Once and for all. He pressed the delete button on all your transgressions. Every one of them.

Even that one.

All that's left for you now is to accept this for the glorious fact that it legitimately and eternally is. In doing this, *you have* forgiven yourself.

You've done well not to let pride downgrade your sin in your own eyes so that you think it's hardly deserving of a slap on the wrist. But seeing clearly the depth of your failure and iniquity, you must let your "godly grief" produce "a repentance that leads to salvation without regret" (2 Corinthians 7:10).

On your knees, with hands outstretched, resolve to receive forgiveness.

His forgiveness.

Click. Delete.

• *Describe in your own words the differences and connections between forgiving yourself and receiving God's forgiveness.*

• *Choose one past action that you've held against yourself, and then prayerfully consider the Lord's payment for this sin. Choose to receive it for yourself.*

No More Circles

A young woman once e-mailed to tell me an odd fact that had led her to a profound observation. Her sister, it seemed, owned a retired circus pony. But even though his days of working the circuit were now over, this little pony did nothing but wander in circles all day. Here he was, in a newfound place of freedom, fully able to range and explore and experience all that his new life had to offer. Yet his old life still haunted him. Defined him. Restrained him. Controlled him. He kept to the same pattern to which he'd been relegated for so long. He apparently didn't know how to operate any other way.

This is the burden of unforgiveness. This is its legacy. It sits on you, weighing you down, restricting you from enjoying the new spaces and phases and freedoms that each season of life brings you. It fits you with blinders, keeping you from seeing anything other than the offense done against you, making it hard to view anything else in your life except through its lens. Unforgiveness forces you to stay one-dimensional, thinly sliced, unable to experience the joys that only exist on the periphery. Instead it keeps you narrowly relegated to the artificial boundaries created by yesterday's disappointments—a circle of mundane living that's far less than the abundant life you were created for.

Ask me how I know.

If we were sitting together right now, I'd be crying right alongside you. What's happened is bad. Terrible. In many ways—in every natural sense—unforgiveable. Perhaps it's still going on, in fact. You've *tried* to forgive. You've *thought* you were there. But then here it comes again— another betrayal, another broken promise, another blow to your fragile trust—and as a result, deeper hurt. Closed loops. Tighter circles. The memories are always near the surface.

I know. I know. Believe me, I know.

But as a wise mentor of mine once told me before he transitioned to heaven, "The entirety of your life is made up of two percentages. Ten percent is what happens to you. Ninety percent is how you react to what happens." Sure, we wish we could control everything and redo much of what's gone on. But the reality is, we can't change it now. In many cases we couldn't have done anything about it when it did happen, even if we'd wanted to. Some of these things may have occurred when you were so young you had no voice or strength to refuse. And without simplifying or minimizing the staggering effects of those tragic offenses, the truth remains that these events and circumstances—the actual moments when they occurred—make up only a small portion or percentage of your life. The much larger portion, the part that really defines the person you're becoming and the life you ultimately create, is the space where you've tried (and still try) to grapple and deal with what's happened.

It's into this 90 percent space that forgiveness falls.

So, again, while not pretending to be a counselor, and not able in this small chapter to discuss everything the Bible says about forgiveness—and certainly not implying that this equates to flipping a switch at 6:30 and enjoying a nice coffee at 6:45—I'm just here to tell you the truth.

I want your abundant life back. No more circles.

Please, God, no more circles.

Forgiveness is reached through a combination of several actions.

First, refuse to store up and harbor a grudge. Make an active decision not to hold a debt over someone else's head or to keep an ongoing record of their wrongdoing. Choose instead to release them of that liability, and then trust God—who knows every detail of everything that's happened—to work on your behalf to bring justice while also bringing healing to your heart, even if not a clean resolution to the problem or a restoration of relationship. Forgiveness means releasing into His hands the person, the circumstance, and the outcome. All of it.

That's the way He did it with us, right?

He forgave all our sins. He canceled the record of the charges against us and took it away by nailing it to the cross. (Colossians 2:13–14 NLT)

This is the framework of forgiveness we are to follow—releasing others from the very real charges we've stacked up against them and freeing them from the debt, whether they've admitted their mistake or not. Learning to discipline yourself not to harbor resentment or continue building your case against them in your mind is a difficult but necessary activity in any victorious Christian's life, which will often require accountability and godly counsel to walk out in daily life. Making this resolution will not only affect the health of your current relationships but will also prepare you to have more stable ones in the future.

- If a wife expects to find joy in marriage, she must be able to quickly forgive her husband when he upsets her.
- If a mother expects to enjoy her children, she must rapidly release any hurt they inflict upon her, not letting it settle inside and fester into resentment.
- If a daughter expects to fulfill the biblical requirement to honor her parents, she must write off any debt she feels owed as a result of her parents' failings.
- If a friend expects to relate with any depth and vulnerability toward another, she must not feel entitled to her well-dusted collection of cataloged offenses.
- If any group in society wants to move forward, building health and prosperity for future generations within that community, this group must forgive, whether or not an apology is made by the one or ones who offended.

Unshackling others from the built-up resentment over issues from the past, or even issues from last night, is not something we do necessarily for their benefit. We do it for ours. It doesn't excuse their behavior; it just frees us up from being held captive to it.

Truly a wounded heart cannot open up either to fully love or receive love. And one who harbors her wounds as some kind of protection against further wounds only tightens the hard places in her heart that keep her locked in circles, never escaping what's happened, stuck in her predictable ruts and reactions.

So I'm urging you to make this first decision. To clear the decks and stop keeping count.

And here's how you'll know you're doing it. If someone does something today that causes you to be angry—which will keep happening sometimes, even after you make this resolution—and you immediately begin rehearsing everything they did yesterday and the day before, you'll know you're still living in unforgiveness. If what this person has just done becomes the cherry on top of a cake you've been baking for days, weeks, and years, you'll know that you still have a tendency to store up offenses.

But as you start releasing them from your debt—and releasing yourself from the burden of carrying it around and keeping up with it—your treatment of them will no longer have their past continually reflected in it. You'll be free. You'll deal in the present. You'll feel like a new person. The air around you won't have that choked, acrid sourness about it.

Your circles will grow wider. Your experiences will take you to more rewarding, more refreshing places. Right away. More each day.

Second, leave room for God to act on your behalf. It's quite natural to feel as though forgiveness lets the other person just get away with it. You're still the victim, and they're still the oblivious, unpenalized offender. You're especially likely to feel this if you never hear this other person express any regret for their actions, or if their lame attempt at an apology is more like a self-justification, trying to shroud *you* in as much or more blame as themselves. Their pitiful way of saying "sorry" only reveals how they obviously still don't get it.

Yes, repentance is an important, necessary step on their part if they're ever to experience freedom from what they've done. That's why

Jesus could say, "If your brother sins, rebuke him, and if he repents, forgive him. And if he sins against you seven times in a day, and comes back to you seven times, saying, 'I repent,' you must forgive him" (Luke 17:3–4). Their acknowledgement of wrong is expected and crucial.

But if they don't, or can't, or won't admit to the harm they've caused you, it's not your job to ensure they get what's coming to them. By giving them your forgiveness, you leave it up to God to deal with them. And deal with them, He will—in His own way, in His own timing, much better and more thoroughly than *you* ever could.

Refuse the urge to retaliate. Trust that He will do your fighting for you. Believe that He will serve your best interests in the circumstances at hand as you stay humble and at peace before Him. By choosing not to fill in every margin with your own well-thought-out plans for restitution, you choose instead to "leave room for God's wrath" (Romans 12:19 NIV).

Finally, pray. It is imperative that you ask the Lord to empower you to forgive. You can't do this in your own strength. You shouldn't expect to. To release others from the debt they owe requires supernatural resources, strengthening, and encouragement. Pray for it. Pray for all of it. And He will respond.

Forgiveness is a miracle. It really is. It's a supernatural outworking of God's Spirit through you, enabling you to extend something you could never do apart from His indwelling activity. He alone can compel a grieving mother to forgive her child's killer, or a betrayed friend to forgive an act of emotional disregard and cruelty, or a deceived wife to welcome back the one with whom she exchanged those first vows.

Only one power, one invisible force, one miracle can clear away the eroding illness that robs you of peace and love and the enjoyment of life. Only one substance is heavy and blanketing enough to douse the raging fire of resentment that burns away your joy, the flames that have left behind nothing but scraps and soot and the ashy remnants of what your life could have been.

Only God can alter your pattern, quicken your step, expand your reach . . . and get you out of those circles.

Again—and again and again—by no means am I suggesting that these steps are simple or easy to do. They frequently require the practical help of wise, discerning, ongoing counsel and therapy. I'm only proposing, by the authority of God's Word, that it is worth it. Being a woman resolved to forgive can save your friendships, rescue your marriage, restore your relationship, rebuild your life, refurbish your business, reestablish your work, and help you regain your very self, allowing you to live freely. Lovingly. With joy.

This is the mission of the resolution at hand. This is its purpose, seeing to it, again, "that no one falls short of the grace of God and that no root of bitterness springs up, causing trouble and defiling many" (Hebrews 12:15). It is designed to rescue you, while bringing with it the added by-product of extending the impact of your grace toward those you love.

Just as the Lord has forgiven you, so you are also to forgive.
(Colossians 3:13)

This is your offering. Extending forgiveness. Just as He has so wonderfully, abundantly, and outlandishly poured it out on you.

Now I'm certain this is not the first thing you've ever read or the first message you've ever heard on the topic of forgiveness. I'm fully aware that this theme and need are as ancient as the Bible itself. There's nothing innovative or particularly brilliant about what I've shared—no formerly unknown secret, no 1-2-3 formula for unlocking yourself from a prison of bitterness.

You've known all this. But what have you done with it?

Have you resolved to be forgiven, as well as to forgive? Taking the steps to do it makes all the difference.

Therein lies the secret you've possibly been waiting to discover— the promised opportunity to change the geometry of your life from endless circles into the best shape your heart has ever been in.

- *Circle the step that's most difficult for you in forgiving someone else, and then consider why that's the case:*

- refusing to store up and harbor a grudge
- leaving room for God to act on your behalf
- praying, asking the Lord to give you a desire to forgive

• *Think of the names you wrote at the first of this section—people you are holding grudges against. Ask the Lord to empower you to forgive them. Then replace the underlined phrase with each person's name, "forgiving <u>one another,</u> just as God also forgave you in Christ" (Ephesians 4:32).*

• *To be fair and complete, is there anyone you need to request forgiveness from? As the Scripture says, "If you are offering your gift on the altar, and there you remember that your brother or sister has something against you, leave your gift there in front of the altar. First go and be reconciled with your brother or sister, and then come and offer your gift" (Matthew 5:23–24) . . . even your gift of forgiveness.*

• *As you move forward to sign this resolution, remember that this should only be the beginning—the initiation of a journey that may take time and counsel to complete. Commit to seeking the necessary help to fully experience the benefits that forgiveness is designed to give.*

❧ MY FORGIVENESS ☙

I will forgive those who have wronged me and reconcile with those I have wronged.

_____

MY INTEGRITY

*A resolution to live with the highest
standards of virtue and purity*

Structural Soundness

Blessed are those whose way is blameless. (Psalm 119:1 NASB)

More than ten years ago when I first began preparing to write a book like this—one that covers a wide range of different topics—it seemed necessary to involve other women in the process. I sent copies of all these resolution points to a selected group of my friends—women from different age groups, ethnic backgrounds, and current life situations—and asked them to prayerfully consider each of these statements and how they intersect with reality. And overwhelmingly, this particular resolution dealing with integrity and personal purity struck some of the deepest chords in women's hearts, challenging and convicting all of us in a way that truly resonated.

I will not tolerate evil influences even in the most
justifiable form, in myself or my home . . .

Even in the most justifiable form. That's the phrase that sort of cut beneath the skin. And it still does even now. It causes a noticeable flinch. Involuntary. Ouch. Most women don't have trouble avoiding (or at least recognizing the problem with) the conspicuously evil things, the outright no-no's. It's those undercover, low-key matters, the ones that cloak themselves in the guise of entertainment—those are the ones that hook us. They're unobtrusive. Quiet. Too comfortable and familiar to be asked to leave. Just there. Justifiable.

Yet when seen in the stark black-and-white of a resolution list like this, they strangely lose their cover and camouflage. Many of the women running their finger along the page suddenly found themselves yanking it back, as if brushing against a hot iron. The burn in their fingertips matched with an eerie chill of conviction down their backs.

No doubt, this point of resolution calls for an intimate, personal, introspective look at what's going on in the quietness of our own hearts and homes. In our DMs and on our devices. In our bedrooms and bathrooms. It touches on some of those allowances we make behind closed doors, in the quiet of our dens and living rooms, where laziness and leniency have been known to hang around after dinner and stay up into the wee hours. That's why, honestly, it often requires a resolution like this before we recognize that these things we've been sanctioning with our time and attention are a glaring contradiction of who we are and what we say we believe.

Once the shock wore off, my group of friends and I agreed. With our lives standing exposed beneath the spotlight of this resolution, out came a parade of confessions about the television shows we've binged, the novels we've lost ourselves in, the profiles we've followed and the comments we've posted, the music we've pumped through our earbuds and car speakers.

Willing to dig a little deeper, one sister awoke to the fact that the fun, friendly connection she was maintaining with an old flame was carrying an undercurrent of emotional infidelity and potential disaster. Another came clean about a stash of wine she deceptively kept in the back of a hallway closet and frequently pulled out to *overindulge* in when no one else was around.

No big deal? Easily justifiable?

But each of these whispered cases of compromise was, on varying levels, dulling and muting the spiritual senses of every woman who admitted to them. Even if just a little bit, these choices were enough to cause a nudge of conscience. If ignored and allowed, they represented even more—a deliberate refusal to grant God access to this area of life, to this two-hour time slot, to this understandable indulgence.

What starts with a sliver becomes a river.

Obviously a lot of the lifestyle choices exhibited and lauded on *this* show or in *that* book are things we would never agree with in person, activities we would never engage in. And while it would be legalistic and impersonal to tell people exactly what types of shows they should or shouldn't watch, exactly what kinds of movies and books they should or shouldn't like, we all know the difference between valuing honest discourse and being entertained by sin. We know when we're not just observing the grittiness of real-life issues but are finding it personally provocative, enjoyable, almost (almost?) desirable. Instead of being repulsed by certain behaviors and grieved at the lies being foisted on our generation, we find ourselves more accepting of them, willing to watch and laugh, considering them suitable viewing with a side of popcorn.

And what does that make us but the hypocrites we never wanted to be. Discouraging one thing in public while finding it addictively exciting in private.

This speaks to the essence of integrity.

Integrity means being the same underneath as we are on the outside. Unimpaired, whole, and sound. It's what the engineer is intent on achieving by designing a bridge that not only *looks* like it can handle the traffic flowing across it but is architecturally able to support the weight of it, day after day, year after year. *Structural integrity.*

That's what we're after.

And that's why this resolution is not for the flippant and faint of heart.

I don't mind admitting, sister, this resolution has caused me to step back and look again at my own life. Don't feel like you're the only one whose toes are feeling stepped on here. I, too, want to be a woman of distinction, marked by God's Spirit. I desire to be the wife, mother, and woman God created me to become. I want my spiritual ears clear to hear His voice, my spiritual eyes unblurred to His presence. I want to be here to receive the peace His presence can bring to my home. I want to experience His power pulsating through our family and ministry.

But I know this type of practical, day-to-day blessing will never coexist with some of the lewd, lascivious nonsense that's spouted from today's most popular media portals. I must realize, as the mother of evangelist John Wesley is said to have written to her son:

> Whatever weakens your reason, impairs the tenderness
> of your conscience, obscures your sense of God, or
> takes off the relish of spiritual things—in short, whatever
> increases the strength and authority of your body over
> your mind—that thing is sin to you, however innocent it
> may be in itself.

Peruse that statement again. Slowly this time. It's okay, take your time. I'll wait.

Remarks like hers call us to a point of decision. We must decide.

Which do we want more?

God's best, or our personal favorites?

Maybe this was the type of bare-bones, bottom-line question that drove King David to resolve so seriously about living a life of integrity:

> *I will be careful to live a blameless life—when will you come*
> *to help me? I will lead a life of integrity in my own home.*
> *I will refuse to look at anything vile and vulgar. . . . I will*
> *have nothing to do with them. (Psalm 101:2–3 NLT)*

This was not the norm for the kings of ancient nations. Powerful and highly unaccountable, these monarchs felt free to live as they pleased anywhere they went, especially within the confines of their personal living quarters. Unchecked. Unbridled. No one had the right to tell them what to do. King David, however, wanted to be different, and he expressed several of the commitments he employed to help him achieve his goal—ones that we can make as well.

1. *Have no tolerance for evil.* "I will refuse to look at anything vile and vulgar," he wrote (v. 3). He was unwilling for anything that went against the standards and statutes of God to be paraded before him as entertainment. He promised not to engage in any activity that could slowly, progressively cause him to be desensitized to sin.

2. *Closely monitor the type of people you allow to influence you.* "I hate all who deal crookedly; I will have nothing to do with them. I will reject perverse ideas and stay away from every evil" (vv. 3–4). No one who was slanderous, proud, or lacking in integrity would be able to live in close relationship with him. He was not about to let their poor character and counsel become a loud, persistent voice in his head or discourage him from the upright path.

3. *Recognize your need for divine help.* "I will be careful to live a blameless life—when will you come to help me?" (v. 2). David knew he could never keep the demands of this resolution in his own strength. Only with God's empowerment and encouragement did he stand a chance against the enemy's wiles and his own fleshly tendencies. Never expect that you can recalibrate the frequency settings on your life without lots and lots of God's help, grace, and shepherding. He will be sure to alert you to changes that need to be made and then will eagerly empower you to carry them out, while providing you with accountability through other members of His church.

These are extreme resolutions, but truth be told, I don't think I've ever met a woman of godly, admirable character—one who in my moments of clearest, most serious thinking I longed to pattern my life after—who was not a person of extreme action and resolutions. Those who enjoy the extra measure of God's blessing and favor, who truly navigate their lives well, are those who discipline themselves in ways that many of us would consider borderline unnecessary. But like David, they've found it necessary to be as extreme in one direction as the culture has chosen to be in the other.

Commitment to this resolution is not designed to thrust a cloak of guilt around your shoulders or to legalistically stamp out every freedom God has given you to enjoy in life. Nor does it grant us permission to impose our personal convictions on others. Not everything that bothers one believer is necessarily forbidden for all. Just because some wouldn't consider it "good" doesn't mean it's worthy of being "slandered" (Romans 14:16). But as you consider your own structural soundness, would you say it's able to bear the weight of your Christian profession? Would it hold up if some of your brothers and sisters in Christ arrived at your door unannounced?

Are you who you claim to be?

If this has been an ongoing question and dilemma for you, as it is for most of us—for *all* of us at one time or another—then do this: commit to being sensitive and responsive to any conviction the Spirit may be impressing on your heart right now in regard to a particular pursuit, decision, or activity. Ask Him to make Himself clear to you. Listen to His promptings. Don't ignore His leadings. But also don't ignore His longing and ability to help you, to empower you, to hold you, and walk with you through the tug and turmoil of every tough choice. Be willing to change your temporary wants for His much better alternatives as He directs you that way through His personal knowledge of you and what He wants to accomplish in you. His goal is not to steal your fun but to position you as a clean, pure, available recipient of His best, most fulfilling blessings.

By His power you can resolve.

By His strength you can walk blamelessly.

By His might you can expect to be a woman who pursues in the dark what she proclaims in the light.

- *In light of what John Wesley's mother wrote to him (page 149), what do you participate in right now that . . .*

  - weakens your reason?
  - impairs the tenderness of your conscience?
  - obscures your sense of God?
  - takes the relish off spiritual things?

The Three Percent Difference

Be on your guard, so that your minds
are not dulled. (Luke 21:34)

Rat poison.

I've never really paid much attention to it . . . until today, when I found out from a friend that most varieties are made up of 97 percent food and only three percent poison. These products lure those nasty rodents by the smell and taste of something they actually like, a delectable treat that tastes good going down. But along with a delicious meal, they also ingest trace amounts of fatal toxins that are enough to end their reign of trash-induced terror. Rats die (and aren't we glad they do) because of a small thread of poison laced within an enticing serving of food.

Three percent.

This is often the way our virtue is stolen. Our integrity compromised. Our hearts hardened. Our spirits desensitized to the things of the Lord. Lured in by something seemingly harmless—an enjoyable form of entertainment, the camaraderie of an initially innocent relationship—but then . . .

Poison.

Strategically hidden, craftily disguised. Underneath the surface, just below radar. We lick our lips and go about our business, thinking that everything's going fine. It may take days, maybe weeks, before we begin to notice. But eventually our spiritual organs start to fail. Our passion quells. Our sensitivity and discernment wane. We lose our gag reflex.

We're dying a slow death.

Three percent at a time.

You've seen this in other people too—maybe someone you know personally, or perhaps a celebrity, sports star, or political figure, someone who obviously had no intention of destroying their lives and careers, but who chased a particular pleasure or experience and ended up in the crosshairs of public embarrassment. Exposed, laid bare, melting in the spotlight of unwanted attention and unintended consequences, they're a picture of the damage that three little percentage points can inflict. You're shocked they'd do this, that they'd throw their lives away for so little.

But is this something the enemy is doing with you? What has he cleverly used to seduce *you* into a web woven too tightly for you to escape, just the way he designed it? Where has he hidden even the smallest dots and deposits of poison, undetected until you suddenly realize the terminal effect it's having on you?

Even on the ones you love.

I'll never forget sitting down to watch the season premiere of a television series I had really enjoyed and kept up with during its opening run the year before. It was good, and I'd been pleasantly surprised at how clean and uncorrupted it was, and I'd eagerly waited for the second season to begin in the fall. On the night it was set to debut, I sat my then three-year-old on the sofa beside me. Settled in. Clicked it on. Just in time to catch the preview highlights, ready to be enthralled. But in less than fifteen seconds, the screen lit up with a raucous sexual scene that took me completely by surprise. Frantically, I snatched at the remote, fumbled for the right button to change the channel. But it was too late. That split-second image had been seared into my little boy's eyes and mind. How could I have let that happen . . . to him?

Now let me say that even when we're trying as hard as we can, our sons and daughters will hear things, see things, and be exposed to things that we wish they hadn't. The cell phones they carry in their hands, if nothing else, have made this a certainty. We all live in a technological age. And even if we hold off on giving them access to it for as long as possible, and even if we are determined to incorporate wise parental boundaries, there are always loopholes and nuances that will catch them (and us) off guard. But if we are not being diligent in the integrity department ourselves, we make it that much easier for the window of polluting possibilities to swing open.

Once it's done—whether by the logical consequences of our actions or by pure accident—we can't undo everything. But we can and should pray that God in His mercy and favor would thwart the Enemy from turning these moments into the makings of a stronghold in their lives or ours. We can boldly ask that any potential, long-term harm and confusion be covered by Christ's blood and dissolved before it takes root and becomes any kind of hindrance. Thankfully, Christ's power can cover that.

Yet the fact that something like this can so easily happen is one reason I think Paul went to such lengths to tell us that "among you there must not be *even a hint* of sexual immorality, or of any kind of impurity, or of greed, because these are improper for God's holy people" (Ephesians 5:3 NIV). Even a slight, indirect glance. Even a trace or suggestion. Even that much is too much for God's people—we who have been made holy through His deliberate act of grace, and who bear the responsibility to protect the tender hearts and minds of those we dearly love.

Three percent is where it starts.

Who knows where it might lead?

And while the first part of Paul's admonishment speaks of "sexual immorality"—a spiritual poison that permeated the culture in which Paul lived—his use of the catchall phrase "any kind of impurity" broadens the scope to all the other polluting activities that need to be completely foreign to the believer's lifestyle. These, he says, have no place in our lives. None. He knew what "even a hint" could do.

"A little leaven," he once said, "leavens the whole batch of dough" (Galatians 5:9).

So if you're serious about this, I'm going to suggest that you do more than just make this promise to God and to yourself. Make it to (and with) others as well. Because try as we might to wage our own integrity battles, this kind of living requires accountability. It just does. In a culture saturated with opportunities to be swayed in opposition to purity, the woman resolved to integrity must be girded about with other sisters who are walking with her, holding her accountable to a holy standard.

I am grateful to the Lord for giving me friendships that provide this accountability framework and network for me. Several of us women enjoy getting together to share one another's lives. We talk. We ask questions. We laugh. We cry. We don't just commiserate. We hold ourselves and one another up to the counsel of God's Word.

On occasion, when we've gone to see a movie, even while sitting there thoroughly supplied with Coke and popcorn, one of us has grown uncomfortable with the direction the film is taking. Caught in a wave of conviction, sometimes *I've* been the one who's needed to slip out for a while. Sometimes we've *all* come to the same conclusion and left as a pack in mid-reel. I don't know how to thank God enough for friends who don't make me feel embarrassed for being spiritually sensitive, who provide me a place where my resolution to live pure before Him is never under pressure, never a point of ridicule, never ganged up against. Our willingness to support one another helps us remain resolved.

We need this.

We can't make it without this.

Because it doesn't take a lot of poison to take us down. Just a small percentage can kill.

But by spreading it out among a whole group of us who are constantly helping each other whittle that 3 percent down to 2, to 1, till it's not "even a hint," we're able to stand strong to our feet again. By living our lives openly before others, we women—both single and married— allow ourselves to be searched and known by another who has our best interest in mind, someone who has a nose for spotting poison. If you don't have an accountability relationship like this, make it a matter of prayer. I believe the Lord will honor your desire and will answer your request. He wants you blessed and pure and peacefully enjoying a life that is fully pleasing and honoring to Him.

- *Is there an area of your life that you'd be embarrassed or ashamed for others to find out about?*

- *How would a deeper, more vulnerable, more comprehensive type of accountability be of use to you in maintaining a high level of integrity? What would that look like, and would you be willing to submit to it?*

From Strength to Strength

In our previous neighborhood, a gorgeous piece of property lay behind our next-door neighbor's house where my boys and I loved to play when they were small. Thankfully, she never minded us showing up and helping ourselves. The thick brush and the wide, tall trees provided a perfect environment for me to kill some afternoon hours with my adventuresome and inquisitive sons.

They found a pathway just up the perimeter that got us around the daunting tree line. We'd enter at that narrow, weathered trail, and then lose ourselves in the curvy pathways of this wooded wonderland, embarking on another timbered escapade. We soon turned into explorers—building forts, ducking under fallen branches, imagining ourselves hiding from hostile enemies in little coves.

This trail eventually wound around to a small, dry creek bed that doubled as the perfect place for many of our imaginary story lines to develop. On one occasion, we became particularly entertained by a large tree that had fallen across the ravine. My kids considered this a thrilling discovery. Each one of my sons, balancing themselves carefully, took turns going across, laughing at one another's bobbles and falls, then celebrating when victory was finally achieved.

I sat down on a patch of dried leaves nearby, entertained. Just watching. Didn't feel the need to get up on that thing myself. But my children wouldn't let me off the hook that easily. They began begging that I participate with them, taking my own turn to balance myself on the log and go from one side to the other.

I finally obliged.

When I first started out, I didn't think it would be that difficult. I had been a bit of a gymnast as a kid, after all. Surely I could walk a few feet on this wide tree trunk—balance beam style—especially with the boys cheering me on.

Everything was going great until I got about midway across and started to hear a tiny cracking sound underneath me. Uh-oh. It didn't take but a couple more seconds before the entire log snapped into pieces and fell crashing into the creek bed. My backside wasn't far behind.

There on the ground, I sat completely stunned. It had all happened so fast. Took me a moment to regain my composure. But after clambering to my feet, dusting myself off, and looking back at the splintered remains of the tree trunk scattered along the ground, it was clear what the problem had been. Despite the tough, thick bark that made it appear so strong and secure on the outside, this fallen log, now with its insides exposed, showed just how rotten it was. Decay and deterioration had set in over time, which was likely what had caused it to collapse in the first place. When the boys walked across it, their tiny bodies hadn't been enough to reveal its weaknesses. But when I stepped onto it with an adult weight, it couldn't bear up. There wasn't enough resiliency on the inside to match its appearance on the outside. Couldn't handle the pressure. Snap. It didn't have . . .

Integrity.

Sooner or later, for all of us, the inevitable pressures of life will reveal the truth of what's inside. Sure, external strength alone can be enough to handle some of the simpler, less demanding situations, but when the stress builds to a certain weight and downward force, when it's more than our surface assets alone can carry, the person lacking depth of integrity will snap. Fall to pieces. Implode. Then everyone can plainly see that underneath the masquerade of strength was a hidden, interior life infested with decay, unattended and uncared for.

And unfortunately, we see way too much of this. Both in ourselves and in others.

But not in everyone. And when we come across a person who defies this depressing trend, we should come closer to observe. Look and learn.

Enter the prophet Daniel.

When he and his talented young friends, along with around ten thousand other Hebrews, were captured by King Nebuchadnezzar and hauled away to Babylon in 605 BC, they were threatened on numerous occasions to change their lifestyle to suit the new surroundings, to become something different from what they knew they'd been commissioned to do as followers of Israel's God. Their handlers, seeking to co-opt their skills and potential for nationalistic purposes, gave them Babylonian names, trained them in Babylonian literature, even sought to reorient their tastes by plying them with Babylonian foods.

Yet even in this new reality, Daniel refused to compromise his standards of holiness. And because no one could help but notice the superior intellect God had given him, including his ability to interpret dreams and visions—surpassing that of even the king's most capable wise men and appointed officials—Daniel was swiftly promoted through the Babylonian ranks into positions of royal influence and service.

Pretty heady stuff for a young Hebrew.

So when the Persian Empire gained control over Babylon, toppling the power structure, Daniel was faced with the prospect of losing his prestigious career and promising outlook. Unless he wanted to risk the newfound stature he'd grown accustomed to, this might be a good time to make at least a few strategic, acceptable compromises away from the values of his upbringing.

He didn't have to wait long for the chance. When a jealous, conniving brood of officials sought to trap him by convincing King Darius to sign a decree commanding that everyone, for thirty days, direct their prayers and petitions only to the king and to no other god—punishable by death in the lions' den—Daniel had to choose. He could lower his standards temporarily, for a month. He could do his real praying in private, not out where everybody else could see it. Lead a double life to save his singular position.

But instead . . .

> *When Daniel learned that the document had been signed,*
> *he went into his house. The windows in its upstairs*
> *room opened toward Jerusalem, and three times a day*
> *he got down on his knees, prayed, and gave thanks to*
> *his God, just as he had done before. (Daniel 6:10)*

He didn't change his standards to suit the new regime.

Didn't reformat his convictions to remain popular and accepted.

Didn't hide his reverence to keep from being found out by others.

Didn't alter his schedule to fold into the new dictates of the king's decree.

Rather, he stayed sure and strong and steady. He remained the same person behind closed doors (and open windows) as he claimed to be on the other side. Even when faced with the ultimate test—the extreme, lip-smacking pressure of the lions' den—he didn't crumble under the stress and strain. He was able to stand courageous in the face of daunting circumstances because he was "found innocent" before the Lord (v. 22).

His integrity saved him.

Kept those lions' mouths closed. Kept him intact, from being torn to pieces. Kept him protected amid mounting adversity.

And it sent a rippling message of the strength of Yahweh throughout the entire land. King Darius was so shocked, overwhelmed, and grateful for Daniel's veracity and Yahweh's response to it that he issued a new decree, recognizing Him as the only true and living God.

The tree trunk of integrity held strong across a ravine of possible disaster. It made all the difference in Daniel's life.

And it will make the difference in yours.

• *Resolving to be a woman of integrity is one of the best gifts you can give yourself. It means you're free! No longer living in fear of a secret life being "discovered" or "found out." By signing and agreeing to this, you are agreeing to line up your whole self with the person God has already rebirthed and transformed you to be. You're also opening yourself to become an influence and example that will draw others around you to Christlikeness.*

❧ MY INTEGRITY ☙

I will not tolerate evil influences even in the most justifiable form, in myself or my home, but will embrace and encourage a life of purity.

_____

MY HEART

A resolution to care

Look Again

Why do You force me to look at injustice?
Why do You tolerate wrongdoing? (Habakkuk 1:3)

I didn't want to see it. The images were too disturbing. The towering HD-quality screen perched overhead translated every single pixel of this devastating story into a larger-than-life reality for me, as well as for the fifteen thousand other women who were assembled there, watching.

We were at a conference in Sydney, Australia, a gathering held once a year and attended by women from every corner of the globe. Olive-skinned Asians dressed in bejeweled saris from India; fair-skinned blondes from Denmark; dark-haired, exotic Russians; black, French-speaking sisters from an exotic island I'd never even heard of before, all before sharing the same space for this momentous affair. The convention, one of the largest of its kind, is intentional in its focus. It's not just a once-a-year experience where you come, do the weekend, then don't really think about it till next time. It has actually become an ongoing, year-round sisterhood—a transglobal connection of women seeking to serve Christ, pursue justice, and change humanity through specific outreach and ministry.

Frankly, this kind of meeting was new for me. Many of the conferences I'd attended up to that point, though always filled with great teaching and amazing worship experiences, didn't normally have a focus on humanitarian efforts. Being in the midst of this type of event was opening my eyes in a whole new way to issues the global community is facing.

And it was convicting.

Because who can deny that this kind of active mercy is what Christ compels His church to do? And if so, why wasn't I doing it? Why wasn't I using the platform the Lord had given me to encourage women to look outside the tight orbits of their own lives and pressing concerns and see the grave suffering around them? Why weren't all of us—from every corner of the globe, even and especially the most prosperous parts—as visibly broken by these gaping needs as believers from other countries seemed to be, some of whose nations and homelands are far less economically stable? These women, far from wanting to come to a conference for their personal edification alone, sensed a responsibility to impact culture as a result—as a goal—of their time together.

Some of the issues presented to us that day were ones I already knew about at some level. Others of them, ten years ago, I had no idea existed, like the one currently flashing across the screen in front of me. But I could tell in an instant that I could no longer feel oddly removed and void of obligation to do anything about it, about such horrors as this.

Pictures of women. Hard to look at. Tortured at the hands of brainwashed child soldiers in Uganda. These hardened kids under the supervision of the LRA (Lord's Resistance Army) had been trained to commit some of the most terrifying, heartless crimes and injustices you can imagine, leaving women wounded and scarred for life, barely able to function in the normal realms of society, their facial features violently marred at the hands of a renegade soldier's razor blade. Plastic surgeons, we were told, were standing ready to help, willing to give of their time, skill, and training. All that was needed now were the resources for travel and medical costs. And we were being commissioned to help.

A steady chorus of gasps and sniffles resonated throughout the vast arena as the video presentation played. Tears streamed down our cheeks. We passed tissues down the rows. So moved, so touched, so traumatized. On more than one occasion, unable to bear any more, I had to lower my gaze momentarily to escape the visual assault.

This just couldn't be real! This kind of thing doesn't really happen. To real people. To mothers and daughters. In their own land. Does it?

When they showed the same clip a second weekend (when the conference was repeated for another influx of attendees), I'll admit—I sneaked out. I just couldn't do it again. Didn't think I could handle another look at those images that gave me such churning emotions, that made me lose my appetite the rest of the day and then kept me up at night nursing the horror of what I'd witnessed.

I didn't want to see.

I didn't want to look.

And maybe you don't want to look either. Perhaps, like this particular issue, the pictures you see (but don't want to see) are of some devastating reality that plagues another part of the world or a faraway people group. Your typical response is to change the channel or keep scrolling in order to look away from the mistreatment, the lack of dignity, the oppression and impoverished squalor, to remain willfully ignorant instead of digging deeper and finding out what's really happening.

Or maybe what you'd rather not see is *not* a world away. Quite possibly it's in your own backyard. In fact, I can assure you it is. Sneaky hints of racism and classism; bias that shows up in the disparity of how certain people are treated; the effects of gentrification in established sectors of town that push longtime residents out of their homes and neighborhoods, unable to afford the rising costs of the "new and improved." And if it's not that, it's something else. Moral decay is creeping in, less and less inconspicuously every year. Escalating, addictive behaviors are stealing the health and futures of people young and old, people who can't seem to get out of their own destructive way. Families are breaking. Children are going hungry. People are hurting and losing hope, overwhelmed by circumstances they see no end to.

And the sight of it—if you and I were truly willing to look at it and take it in—would make our stomach turn into tightened knots. We know that. Our emotions could barely stand one more minute of this reality—these scenes flashing before us—a story we've noticed but have not really wanted to think about, care about, or do anything about.

Until now.

Until this resolution.

For even though you can't be humanly responsible for everything you see, and even though God would never place the burden of the whole world on your shoulders, He is placing *this* circumstance there, into your spiritual sight line and into your heart. Whatever *it* is. And in prayer He may be saying to you that one small part of its solution is staring you in the face when you step up to the bathroom mirror in the morning.

Listen, I totally understand why you—why I—would rather look away. I understand our tendency to feel like somebody else will surely take care of this. "It's so much easier not to care" is how a close friend of mine described it. It's always easier, less weighty, and far more comfortable to pull back and disengage, to find something more pleasant to dwell on, to skip through life as if it isn't a problem because it isn't your problem. We can feel like the biblical prophet Habakkuk when, after seeing deplorable things happening that he didn't want to see, turned toward the heavens and asked, "Why do you force me to look?" (1:3).

Seems like a God who loves us so fiercely wouldn't mind giving us a break from all this. Seems like with all we're required to shoulder in our own lives, with our own schedule and all our demanding circumstances, He'd give us a pass to look away, to ignore, to disregard. Right?

Almighty God's answer to Habakkuk's question may surprise you. For after forcing the prophet to sit back and watch the suffering of his own beloved people, here's what God said to him.

> *Look . . . ! Observe! Be astonished! Wonder! Because*
> *I am doing something in your days—you would*
> *not believe if you were told. (v. 5 NASB)*

Look intentionally.

Observe it deliberately.

In other words, seeing is believing.

If God didn't show you, your heart would not be moved. You wouldn't be touched with empathy for others that galvanized you into action. You wouldn't be able to grasp the full depth and height of the problem or what the touch of His supernatural care, kindness, and wisdom could accomplish through you. If He allowed you to turn your face away and remain unaware of the situation, you'd never know the outworking of compassion the Spirit of God is inviting and empowering you to experience.

So He's decided to show you—to let you *see* the chaos, the devastation, the damage, the ruin, the waste, the loss—preparing you to envision how stunning His work can be, even through the likes of ordinary people like you and me.

So don't stop looking. Don't turn your eyes away. What you're seeing, He has orchestrated for you to see. In His sovereign plan for your life, He is calling you, wooing you, compelling you to get involved.

Light is brightest against the backdrop of darkness.

Diamonds are most brilliant against a backcloth of black velvet.

Look. Again.

Until what takes your breath away is not the gravity of the problem but the power of God to heal it—one touch, one person at a time.

- *What recent global or local devastations are you currently seeing that stir compassion in your heart?*

- *How would you describe your usual response to seeing such uncomfortable realities? Self-righteousness and self-preservation? Defense of yourself and your own vantage point? Dismissiveness to the point of callousness? Or do you more often feel compassion, drawn toward being willing to help, to learn from those who are expressing their hurt and concern?*

- *If you have remained detached, what has kept you from doing something to help?*

- *What is one thing you can do and would be willing to make time to do?*

How Do You Heal an Unbroken Heart?

When the video clip was over, no one moved.

Everyone, including me, sat glued to her seat, unable quickly or easily to digest what we had just seen. The conference host took a moment to collect herself before continuing on with the program.

It was indeed a *moment*.

I bet you know what I mean by that—one of those rare glimpses of supernatural invitation when you just know God's presence is hovering, inviting, impressing upon you a sense of His specific call. We all knew for sure that our hearts would never again be the same. How could they? We couldn't be stirred this deeply and then just move on with our lives as if nothing had happened. We were sure—I was sure—that if we were truly concerned with helping others get to heaven, we'd better be equally concerned about the quality of their existence on earth.

The days of my ministry being relegated to teaching from a platform or writing books were over. That just wasn't enough. If we weren't deliberately, purposefully resolved to help people in practical ways and encourage others to do the same, we would be forever lopsided, guilty of doing only half of what God's people have been called to do.

I bowed my head before the Lord, unsure of what to say to Him exactly. So I just asked—asked Him what He'd have me do in response to this internal gnawing I sensed from His Spirit. And before His answers could even begin taking shape in my mind, the praise team took the stage, their chorus ringing out as if preparing the way for His response:

> Break my heart for what breaks yours
> Everything I am for your kingdom cause
> As I walk from earth into eternity[1]

There it was. The first hints of God's answer to me. I needed a heart that was broken. Not just to *allow* it to break but to *ask* Him to intentionally break it. I needed to be offended and heartsick over the same things that touch the heart of the Father. Instead of sticking to my normal line of prayer requests, basically asking Him *not* to allow my heart to be broken, I was to ask Him to shatter it—until all that was left was that which made me follow Him in the direction He wanted me to go.

So, yes, I was supposed to act. In what way I wasn't yet sure. But before I could know, and before I could go, I needed a broken heart.

Have you ever asked Him for that? Have you ever considered that any disinterest you may feel in serving and caring and getting your hands dirty might really be because you've never set your heart before Him and mustered up the bravery to ask Him to break it, to make it more sensitive to the ailments of others? Most often we're asking Him to heal it, strengthen it, or restore it. But what kind of supernatural power are we choosing to avoid experiencing by not having a heart broken for the plights of those around us?

Jesus had one. A broken heart.

Throughout the Scriptures we see the portrait of a Man who didn't walk blindly down the dusty, ancient roads of His day, bypassing human devastation and need without a second glance. Rather, He paid close attention. He was moved with compassion. He stopped to care for those who were disenfranchised and distressed, oppressed and hungry, captive and widowed (Psalm 146:7–9).

- When He saw the hungry, His heart was broken (Matthew 15:32).

- When He saw the sick, His heart was broken (Matthew 14:14).
- When He saw the emotionally devastated, His heart was broken (Luke 7:13; John 6:35).
- When He saw the lonely and spiritually lost, His heart was broken (Matthew 9:36)

And when He wasn't *extending* compassion, He was *talking* about compassion—telling stories, giving reminders, pointing people in that direction.

Listen to me now. Showing mercy toward others was an important part of the gospel He came to offer. Calling out injustice and seeking to right it is not an aside to the good news; it is in perfect alignment with it. Jesus didn't turn a blind eye to people's physical needs in order to get to the "more important" spiritual one, and neither should we.

You and I are to be women resolved to do the same. We are part of the church—His church—God's answer for the desperation of our time. If we only attend women's conferences, read encouraging books, listen to sermons, sing worship songs, and yet do little if anything to help others in a tangible way, we relegate our demonstration of His gospel to an impotent, watered-down, self-absorbed exercise.

And while I hope you do all these things and benefit greatly from them, I also pray that you sense a little dissatisfaction that causes you to seek something more—something with an outward focus. And when you see the hurt revealed in someone else's comments or countenance, I pray that you'll express empathy. Loudly, intentionally, and actively.

The Lord saved you for many reasons, but one of them is so that others can sense His compassion manifested toward them through you in practical and concrete ways. Not in words or posts or hashtags only. Definitely not in silence and blank stares. But in deed. In action.

I have a lifelong friend whose whole life and ambitions changed when God broke her heart. Titia moved to Atlanta to pursue the career of her dreams, sacrificing a lot to make this shift. Little did she know it would require more than she ever imagined, including the security of owning a home or having any sure-fire place to lay her head.

One meeting after another fell through. One opportunity after another fizzled and failed. One potential lead after another turned sour. Before she knew it, she was sleeping in her car. Nowhere to go. Nowhere to live. She was effectively homeless, and the daily realities of this lifestyle made her painfully aware of the emotional and physical toll it can have on a person.

She was now meeting people who were experiencing the same predicament, many of whom were hardworking people just like her but who had hit a rough patch from which they couldn't recover. She interacted with single mothers and fathers, ex-business owners, twenty-something high school graduates and disabled vets.

And then, something happened. Her heart woke up to a calling and ministry that has become the focus of her life. Her nonprofit outreach organization *Where Are You?* was founded in 2017, and through this ministry to the homeless she infuses hope into discouraged lives. She feeds displaced families and focuses on helping them forge a pathway to a different existence. She has been a beautiful example to all of us who know her.

She is living out of a broken heart. And people all around her are finding life because of it.

Jesus didn't just *preach* a gospel; He lived one. And now you are His hands and feet—hands that are for more than writing personal checks, feet that are for more than walking to church or to the mailbox so that someone else can be resourced to go. Sending help is honorable. Do it. People and outreach organizations need it. But hiding beneath the cloak of giving keeps you from experiencing the benefits of being the helper God is commissioning you to be.

Right from your own home.

With your own personal resources.

Using the gifts of your own family.

Organizing the unique qualities of your circle of friends.

When Jesus felt empathy toward others, it wasn't a clichéd emotion. It was a deep, gut-wrenching reaction that, according to many commentators, would affect Him physically—the equivalent of having an uneasy stomach. How did He choose to respond to that? He didn't go home, hoping that a good nap would cause His sadness and irritation to wear off. He took His broken heart as a sign to do something, to act in accordance with the Father's will. He went. He served. He listened. He healed.

So . . .

What tugs at your heart?

What causes your stomach to feel uneasy?

Again, it may be an issue affecting people on the other side of the globe. Or it may be a situation involving some neighbors across the street or in the town directly adjacent to yours. It may require a long-term commitment or just a couple of hours on one solitary afternoon. It could be an older woman or a newborn baby. A person from a different background and culture or one similar to your own. Opportunities to serve others come in all shapes and sizes—none more valuable than another. But when you see the one that's yours to do something about, He will cause your heart to be stirred, drawn to an individual and her need, drawn to a family and their pain, drawn to a group of people and their challenges, drawn to a country and their crises.

Take that as your cue to respond, like a woman resolved to compassion.

You may be a person who's not normally moved or emotionally stirred, who just doesn't usually respond that way. And yet you can have the same thing Jesus had—a divine compassion for that which breaks the heart of God and tunes you into His purposes for you. When your heart melts to the touch of searing realities that others are facing, you're experiencing something your sanctification is designed to achieve. You are being changed into Christ's image. Breaking your heart. And in being broken, you're being called to respond, to be humble enough to enter into someone else's experience, to recalibrate your perspective and contribute in a meaningful way.

Yes, you can have it—a godly sympathy that leads to action. You *must* have it. Because your world is waiting to experience Christ through you. *You* are the solution the problem is waiting for. This is why your heart is hurting. This is why it's so hard for you to look. This is the reason your tummy churns at the sight of it.

This is compassion.

So ask the Lord to break your heart, to reveal a need in all its horrible actuality until He gives you the courage to respond.

What is causing your heart to break?

This is your cue.

Do something.

- *Perhaps you've been burned when trying to reach out intentionally. People have taken advantage of you or misunderstood your motives. But when you go to minister Christ's love to another person, what is your real reason for going? What's a better way to evaluate your success than with measurable, feel-good results alone?*

Mercy Me

I've been on a search my entire life. After accepting Christ at an early age, and then growing in my understanding through the years of what it meant to be a Christian, I began to wonder what His will for me was. I knew He had a purpose, one that He hadn't just concocted on the spur of the moment, one that He had carefully crafted beforehand (Ephesians 2:10), before I was even born. But I often felt like it eluded me, as though it was always just out of reach and out of sight. As a younger woman, when I was navigating which subjects to study, which opportunities to accept, and which direction to pursue, I regularly wished that God would be more clear, more forthright, more plainly obvious about what He wanted me to do at that particular point in life.

Maybe you're wondering the same thing. In one area or another, you feel like you're just meandering, weaving aimlessly through your weeks and months, walking around with a continuous question mark floating above your head. You *want* to be in His will, but you just aren't clear what His will is. And so you wait. And keep waiting. Waiting for Him to make His will known so you can get busy doing it.

Admirable desire, my friend.

But what if the disclosure of His continued purposes for your life is at least partly dependent on your obedience to what He's *already* set before you? What if He wants to see your level of faithfulness in responding to what you *do* know before He fills you in on what you *don't*? It's like your child trying to get you to make plans for tomorrow when he hasn't yet taken care of his responsibilities for today. "We'll worry about *later*, young man, young lady, once you've taken care of right *now*." Isn't that the way it goes?

Well, maybe the same idea applies in God's revelation of His will to *us*. For, yes, while some of what He retains in store for you and me is not yet known to us, some of it He has *clearly* and *explicitly* expressed. Case in point:

> *He has showed you, O man, what is good.*
> *And what does the LORD require of you?*
> *To act justly and to love mercy and*
> *to walk humbly with your God. (Micah 6:8 NIV)*

Doesn't get any clearer than that. "He has showed you." Never again can you say that you don't know what He "requires" of you, what His current will is for your life. Sure, there's much more to unfold, an array of details left to discover. But this much you *do* know:

1. Do justice.
2. Love mercy.
3. Walk humbly with your God.

So, sister, I ask you . . . are you doing *that*? Are you making the deliberate and conscious resolution to respond to what you absolutely know God has asked you to commit to? There's no better time to make this resolution than right this minute—to walk away with enough insight about these three imperatives to be able to make some practical decisions on how you're going to live them out.

Justice. A term that, without careful thought, can easily be dismissed as a buzzword, its impact dampened by overuse. But justice is too important to glaze over or casually glance at. In fact, it is so critical that when describing the throne of Almighty God, the psalmist wrote, "Righteousness *and* justice are the foundation of your throne"

(Psalm 89:14). To highlight righteousness without giving equal credence to justice is to prescribe to an imbalanced, distorted view of the Father's nature and being, to His plan and His purposes. And yet many Christians, whether intentionally or not, tend to emphasize one of these twin pillars more than the other.

In Micah's writing, I'm immediately struck by the verb that precedes the call to pursue justice: "to act." Some versions say, "to do." We normally think of "justice" as some ethereal idea, an abstract thought. It's not so much an "act" as just a thing. *Justice.* But in this case justice is an action, something to be manifested and demonstrated. Kindness is beautiful and it matters. But kindness is not the same as justice. Justice requires accountability and a reversal of that which is unjust. Maybe a quick look back at what Micah had to say about Israel's ill-natured activities will help:

> *What sorrow awaits you who lie awake at night, thinking up*
> *evil plans. You rise at dawn and hurry to carry them out, simply*
> *because you have the power to do so. When you want a piece*
> *of land, you find a way to seize it. When you want someone's*
> *house, you take it by fraud and violence. You cheat a man of his*
> *property, stealing his family's inheritance. (Micah 2:1–2 NLT)*

A woman resolved to justice is counter-cultural in her treatment of and interaction with others. She doesn't take advantage of people, even if she has the means and opportunity to do so. She determines instead to act rightly—to pursue a just solution—to deliberately consider the best way people or circumstances could be served in a particular situation. She dearly wants and diligently works for the highest good of everyone involved.

To be clear, she's not a pushover; she's not easily fooled. She's just not looking to get one over on people, swinging things so that she comes out the big winner. And when she sees an injustice that's occurred at the hands of others, she is not silent. Instead she speaks the truth in love, holding people accountable for their actions. Her primary interest is seeing justice done, seeking solutions that come down on the side of truth, ones that are fair, reasonable, objective, and—most importantly—expressive of the love of Christ.

Does this describe you? Do you have a pattern of being more concerned about covering yourself than caring what happens to somebody else? Do you discount the ills and injustices that others express, simply because those issues have not been your own experience? Do you speak up when you see the scales imbalanced, tilted toward injustice, even when it's unpopular within your sphere of influence to do so? Are you more committed to getting the best end of the deal than making sure others are well cared for? Do you fight for justice or just for yourself?

If so, resolve to do better.

Do justice, and . . .

Love mercy. The original word used here for "mercy" can easily be translated "kindness." To "love mercy" means to have a hearty interest in doing things that bless and impact others' lives. It means considering their needs above your own, not because they necessarily deserve it but simply because you "love" doing it for them.

This is what God's mercy looks like toward you and me, doesn't it? He has chosen not to give us what we deserve. Instead of pouring out the rightful judgment and punishment we deserved, He poured it out on His willing Son. Now that our sins are covered by Someone other than us—what mercy!—He graciously showers us with affection, tenderness, and forgiveness. Like Christ, who was willing to stand in the gap for us, we should be willing to do gracious things for others even when their actions and past choices don't necessarily warrant it. Just because.

Mercy, we know, comes with dozens of applications for home, work, church—for every place your daily travels take you. But perhaps nowhere is mercy more clearly seen in your life than in the out-of-the-way places where life *doesn't* take you unless you're deliberately going there, places you have to be looking for to find. Places that demand you to burst the bubble of your own comfort, enter into someone else's experience, and invest some sweat equity, to dirty your hands more than perhaps you usually do.

A commitment like this could take you to uncomfortable areas of town where *they* live, to the schools and stores and churches where *they* go. The places where no one you know wants to go. This kind of heart was descriptive of the well-known Proverbs 31 woman. "Her hands reach out to the poor, and she extends her hands to the needy" (v. 20). She reaches. She extends. It's her initiative. Jesus later said this merciful motivation is indicative of any person whose relationship with Him is pure and genuine. The way we relate to the marginalized and helpless—the "least of these" (Matthew 25:31–46)—bears a direct correlation to our commitment toward Christ Himself.

Using this kind of barometer, then, what would your mercy quotient reveal about your relationship with God? Are you always keeping records to determine what people deserve from you? Do you only give what you feel like they've earned the right to receive? Or are you instead willing to give to those who don't ask, who aren't exactly noticeable, or who could never pay you back?

This is what a woman who extends mercy looks like. It's what you can look like. A woman of justice, mercy, and . . .

Humility. Put the two together—justice and mercy—and what do you get? A woman walking "humbly" with her God. Correctly assessing her own value. Not seeing herself too highly, of course, but not too lowly either. Just pursuing the will of God by daily, faithfully trusting that what He's said and commanded of her is worth her doing her very best. And whenever He's ready to share more through the application of His Word and the voice of His Spirit, she'll be right there ready to receive it. And respond to it.

So with this much strength of character and fullness of life to experience, why have we so often chosen to discount or ignore these written instructions from God while still searching frantically for "His will for my life"?

Could it be that it messes with our sheltered, self-absorbed, "American-dream" lifestyles? Are we concerned that taking this resolution to heart might lead to an uncomfortable change we aren't willing to make, one that requires us to pare down our excesses in order to free up time and finances that could go toward meeting the needs of others? And yet this is at the heart of the gospel we claim to believe. It is what "the LORD requires" of us. How, then, can we say that we want to be in God's will if we conveniently ignore this very clear part of it?

One author wrote about a time when he was convicted by this. He was leisurely reading an essay in which the writer was explaining "the process by which words lose their meanings, and he casually offered that the best example of this phenomenon was Christians: *'Christians, he observed, seem to have the amazing ability to say the most wonderful things without actually believing them.'*

"What became more disturbing," the author continued, "was his list of things that Christians actually say—like, blessed are the poor and humble; it's better to give than receive; judge not, lest you be judged; love your neighbor as yourself, etc.—and examining, one by one, how differently I would live my life if I actually believed such things. As [the writer] concluded, *'The sayings of Christ coexist passively in their minds, producing hardly any effect beyond what is caused by mere listening to words so amiable and bland.'"*[2]

How challenging! And how true.

If we really believe the gospel that Christ came to preach, then we will live like it—even if it means dealing with the discomforts His commands may cause.

Maybe as you come upon the signing of this next resolution, you're already aware of what the Spirit is compelling you to do. Your heart is burning. Compassion is rising up within you. You could put your finger on the person or people He is asking you to show kindness toward, to seek justice for.

The woman who lives under the overpass you see every day on your way to work.

The neighbor whose soldier-husband recently came home wounded from his current mission. She's now a caregiver not only for her three young daughters but also for her disabled companion.

The black or brown mother who feels great concern about the well-being and safety of her young son.

The teenager, pregnant for the second time, who's been ostracized by her family and really needs a shoulder to lean on.

The gay coworker who's given judgmental Christians all the chances she's willing to give them to treat her with dignity, even if they disagree with her choices.

Don't think of yourself first and all the ways you may disagree with their perspectives, politics, and choices—some of which may legitimately be wrong. But ask God to give you His eyes to see them the way He does, and then to equip you to be a beautiful reflection of Him—full of grace *and* truth—even as you stand firm in your allegiance to His Word.

Engaging others and expressing love toward them may require a significant investment of time, energy, and resources—extras you don't feel like you can give. It will most certainly require that you emerge from the confines where you feel most comfortable. But if God births in you the compassion to help, He will also multiply in you the means to handle it.

This should be cause for great excitement because your commitment to obey God in this way could be the key that unlocks the door, inviting Him to reveal His plans for you in other areas and dimensions. This is your opportunity to know His will—imagine that: *knowing God's will*—then doing it without reservation.

That's a woman walking justly, mercifully, humbly with her God.

Learn to do right.
Seek justice.
Defend the oppressed.
Take up the cause of the fatherless.
Plead the case of the widow.
(Isaiah 1:17 NIV)

- *This is your chance to put your faith into action. To BE the gospel instead of just professing it. To confirm what God has been writing on your heart. You may not know exactly who God will call you to serve or how He will supply the resources to meet their need, but you are resolving to be available. To keep your eyes and heart open—and full of justice, mercy, and compassion.*

❧ MY HEART ☙

I will pursue justice, love mercy, and extend compassion toward others.

_____

Part
III

THIS IS WHAT MATTERS TO ME.

HONORING MY HUSBAND

*A resolution to be the kind of woman
who truly blesses her man
(Single? Keep reading. *Wink)*

Marriage Proposal

Twenty-two years ago, I walked down the aisle of my childhood church and joined my life to Mr. Jerry Shirer—for better or worse, for richer or poorer. The days and months leading up to the occasion were filled with all the eager anticipation and planning that is customary for a young couple on the cusp of a new life together. My mother, sister, and I dove into the preparations with gusto, doing our best to really take the time to enjoy all the pre-wedding pleasures.

I'd have to say though, in hindsight, one event during this process stands out most distinctly in my mind. And now, all these years later, I can see it more clearly and understand it more fully than I did back then.

Five weeks before my wedding day, while I was floating around dreamily on cloud nine, a dear friend called and asked if she could take me out for lunch. I enthusiastically agreed. I dressed up in a cute little outfit and arrived with an empty stomach and a full heart, ready to celebrate with a glass of sparkling cider and a delectable entrée.

But when I got there, I could tell the mood wasn't as festive as I'd been expecting. Sure, we had fun. But I knew that something else was on my friend's mind. She hadn't extended this invitation just so we could talk about flowers and bridesmaid dresses. She'd come with something far more serious to discuss.

Fairly early in the meal, in fact, she looked up from her full plate and asked me the question that was pressing on her mind, the question she'd brought me here to ask: *"Are you sure this is what you want to do?"*

Girl, what? I was startled. I'd just selected a cake flavor and marked the final alterations on my bridal gown. *This* was not an appropriate question.

Now lest you get the wrong impression, let me assure you that this friend of mine loved my fiancé. They had become great friends in the short time they'd known each other, and she thought he'd be a wonderful husband for me. She was also thoroughly convinced that Jerry and I genuinely loved each other.

It's just that she . . . was married.

And that can change the way "married" looks.

No longer blinded by the butterflies and wistful illusions of romantic splendor, she had a much different take on the subject than someone in my position might have. She wasn't miserable, just realistic. She was still enjoying a lot of the things single women look forward to in marriage and a husband. But there were also a lot of other things— things that can creep up and surprise a new bride quicker than she can dry-clean her wedding dress and hang it back up properly in the closet.

Well, I didn't know exactly how to answer her. "Was I sure this is what I wanted to do?" *Of course*, I was sure. I wouldn't have said yes to him if I wasn't. But before I could finish my first few stumbling attempts at answering, she asked me a second question: "If he never does anything different, if he never changes or becomes anyone other than the man he is right now, can you love him, honor him, and commit yourself to him for the rest of your life?"

What did she want from me?

She wanted me to hear the truth. She wanted to shoot straight enough with me that when I eventually came down from cloud nine, I'd land on square one. She wanted me to see that marriage requires a full investment of myself to this union. I couldn't just say, "I do" unless I "really did"—unless I wanted to make this partnership and this man my priority. I couldn't go into marriage thinking only about how much he was going to do for *me*. Any chance at having a healthy marriage also required that I think proactively about how I would serve him, esteem him, build him up, and honor him. Was I ready to give the time and energy, the emotional effort and attention that would be required of me as his wife? Would I be willing to make his satisfaction a priority—not at the expense of my own, but as part of what truly satisfies me? And would I maintain it as a priority, even at those times when I felt like he didn't deserve it?

That's what her loaded question was looking to uncover. And that's why it was important for her to ask it of me *before* I became a Mrs.

That's what friends do. They make you put the bubbly juice down long enough to ask the tough questions that require you to think clearly about the path you're walking and where it's likely to take you.

So, since we're friends, I've got to talk to you plainly. I need to ask you a few questions that are well worth the emotional effort involved in answering them honestly.

First I'm wondering, if you're single, whether you think about marriage in this light. I'm curious to know if you've considered the selflessness that would be required of you in becoming a key source of fulfillment and satisfaction for your husband, in assisting him in accomplishing the work God has put him on earth to do.

And I wonder, if you're married, what you've chosen to do with the truth of what my friend was telling me five weeks short of my wedding—the truth you've certainly discovered numerous times, no matter how many years you're already in.

Any woman resolving to fulfill her husband must consider the mysterious facets about him and understand that a major part of her role in marriage will be to value, support, honor, and encourage him, even when it goes against every last nerve impulse in her body. It's the gift you commit to give him when you marry him—to provide a soft place for him to fall when he feels discouraged by his own faults and intimidated by the world's pressures. You are committing to be *for* him even when you'd rather be *against* him. You are determining to be faithful to him, pledging to reserve physical and emotional intimacy only for him.

More than two decades now into my marriage to Jerry, and having watched up-close the marriages of other friends and family, I approach this section with a more knowing, nuanced respect for the layered realities that married life can present. I've walked with a number of women through extremely challenging situations in their marriage, some relationships that were physically or emotionally abusive enough that the healthiest thing they could do at the time was get away from it as quickly as they could.

The marriage relationship can be difficult. Perhaps in your case, *difficult* may not come close to communicating the struggles your husband has brought to your relationship. Depending on what's happening or not happening in your marriage, this may be the one resolution point that makes you want to slam down this book and go find one that's a little more in touch with reality.

I am not minimizing for one minute what you may be going through right now by thinking that a few simple chapters on what you can bring to your marriage will automatically solve everything you're facing. I am well aware how daunting a challenge it might be for you to take me up on this resolution when perhaps you're married to a man who's made none of his own. No way am I pretending this is a piece of wedding cake.

But the fact remains, this resolution is an admirable, biblical aspiration worth pursuing no matter what state you may find yourself in today—even if you're unhappy right now in your relationship—even if you're being tempted to seek satisfaction in another person—even if you are single and hoping to become a wife one day—even if your marriage doesn't end up making it past the latest breaking point. *You* want to be fulfilled, don't you? You want your deepest needs met. Well, your husband wants the same thing. No, he may not be fulfilling his side of the bargain at the moment. But remember, this book is not about him. The reality is, you cannot change him. But you can pinpoint some changes in yourself, and then you can bring that new resolve to your marriage. *You* can be faithful. That much you *can* do. You can be sure that no matter how this story of yours unfolds, and no matter what your testimony will be, you can say with confidence that you sought to honor God—and your husband—in this union. Not perfectly, but purposefully.

I, like you, am on a journey—still learning and growing as I experience daily life with Jerry. And yet observation and personal testimony are teaching me that this resolution will often result in good things for your relationship. That's because spouses tend to live up to the standard they see in those around them, as well as the esteem they receive from their mate. So see if you can make this deal with me in your heart. Overlook what you feel your husband deserves or has earned by his behavior, and simply consider your own personal part in light of this resolution and what it's asking you to commit yourself to do.

You may not want to do it, but I'm asking you a question: *Will you join me in making this resolution anyway?* Not only for your own sake or even your husband's but because doing so will bring honor and glory to the name of the Lord.

- *What are some things you would say if you were counseling a young woman on the eve of her wedding day?*

- *List some of your husband's characteristics that you wish would change but likely will not. Now prayerfully consider how the Holy Spirit may be leading you to adapt your attitudes or reactions to your husband's characteristics if these attributes are never altered.*

- *Before reading further, record some of the facets of your marriage you would like to see affected by this resolution. Use this as a guideline for prayer and a barometer for change in your relationship as you incorporate into your marriage the principles we will discuss.*

- *Single woman, as you read these chapters, take the opportunity to record your thoughts, questions, and insights.*

Hopes and Fears

This whole topic of fulfilling your husband contains more layers than you and I could ever hope to cover in-depth in these few pages. Your husband could probably tell you many things that would help him feel more secure, loved, and fulfilled, and I hope you'll take this resolution as the perfect opportunity to ask him. He is full of emotional needs and (Lord knows) some physical ones that you and I could spend hours talking about together, but it wouldn't be nearly as beneficial and specific as *you and your man* having that discussion. So instead of even trying to cover this topic in full, my hope is that this resolution will at least point you in the right direction in one specific area—one which, as it turns out, has an enormous effect on your husband's feeling fulfilled and encouraged as a man. By you.

(Single sister, you're smart to stay tuned and hang in there with us. Trust me, you'll want to hear this too.)

I've enjoyed the distinct honor of sharing a platform with two beloved authors and Bible teachers—Kay Arthur and Beth Moore. During one of those panel discussions, we sat together on stage as Miss Kay summarized a huge dose of marriage reality into so tight a capsule that any of us could swallow it and keep it down.

She said that men (husbands in particular) possess two great fears:

- the fear of being found inadequate
- the fear of being controlled by a woman

. . . which stir in them several innate desires. Your man wants to be your hero. He wants to feel like he is worthwhile to you and needed by you. He desires more than anything to see a look of love and admiration in your eyes. He wants to know that you celebrate him, depend on him, feel privileged to be married to him, and expect great things from him.

It's okay.

Take a deep breath.

Now promise me you'll keep reading.

Providing this kind of affirmation for our spouses can be hard. I understand. Sometimes a wife's frustration level with her husband can run fairly high, given the current challenges they're facing in a particular season of life. In some marriages the wife's anger and resentment toward him is off the charts, resulting in knee-jerk, emotional flare-ups that are inappropriate ways of responding to what is simply the flawed humanity in her husband. In other cases, the overreaction almost seems warranted. And maybe is. You feel like his little wants and fears can just go take a number. He's given *you* enough wants and fears for the both of you.

So whether this subject sounds interesting to you as you try helping your husband unearth the God-given potential you know is inside of him, or whether it sounds outright infuriating to you based on the track record he's shown you so far, I believe it's something we all need to hear. Because even though a lot of things get brought inside the house and locked into the carpet fibers of our marriage, we do neither our husbands nor ourselves any favors by thinking those stains are coming out on their own. This chapter—this resolution—is our opportunity to get out the spray bottle and the scrub brush and get to work doing something that may just lift some of the deepest, most ground-in dirt from our hearts and our marriage. And even if not everything comes out and cleans up the way we'd hoped, we'll be honoring the Lord by honoring His Word and His purposes for our lives and for this vital relationship.

So let's explore these twin fears in our men's lives and discover what they have to do with us, as well as what could happen if we try to alleviate them.

1. *His fear of inadequacy.* Your husband is capable, honorable, and worthy of your attention and admiration. He desires more than anything to know that you trust him, that you believe he has the wisdom and talent to succeed. He is fulfilled when he senses, despite his inadequacies, that you see the possibilities and potential God has given him as your provider and protector. He likes knowing you're praying for him, rooting for him, and assuring him that he still has what it takes to be the man of your dreams. When he feels genuinely affirmed by you, it makes him want to live up to your trust in most cases. Even when he falls short, his reaction to his own failing—if he knows you're truly supportive of him—will make apparent that his desire was to meet your expectations. You'll see in his eyes that he was trying to please you.

This alone should be some cause for your continued trust and appreciation, as opposed to blanket disapproval (which we are often notorious for offering). When he starts to sense that all you ever think he can do is to be sloppy, forgetful, unimaginative, irresponsible, weak, indecisive, and clueless, he will become less inclined and motivated over time to prove you wrong. He knows you'll only find something to be critical of anyway.

I know your man's not perfect. Not even close, you say? *He knows it too. He's not delusional.* He knows he's flawed, even if he's not quick to admit it out loud. But just like you and me, he is not to be defined by his imperfections. He has been divinely wired to be a leader, father, and provider for your family. And the last thing he needs or wants is a wife who doesn't believe it, who's always correcting him, unwilling to either recognize or support these qualities in him.

A voice of support, confidence, and encouragement from you is *electric* to him. It quells the continual struggle against any sense of inadequacy that smolders inside of him. When you pull him aside to pray for him, when you tell him he's been on your mind, when he sees in your eyes that you're proud of the man he's becoming, it's like a shot of pure adrenaline to his system. It's the soft warmth of security that comforts him from the ridicule of a harsh world and the internal jeering of his own insecurity. Sure, there are times for talking plainly and honestly about things he needs to improve and watch out for. But probably not right now in the heat of the moment with that disappointment written all over his face. And probably not until he already knows for sure that your basic default is to love and take delight in him. An overall demeanor of gratitude will go a long way whenever the occasional reality check is called for.

If you're like me, you have an inclination to be overly critical of your husband's actions. But if your husband is anything like mine (and I suspect he is), he bristles at being corrected, criticized, and mothered by you. It makes him feel belittled and insignificant. Beaten down and discouraged. And even if you think that's the way he *ought* to feel about himself after what he's done and not done for you and your marriage, this sets a man up to be even more damaging and destructive to his entire family. It's not good for anybody.

Men, honestly, even with all their complexities, are really very basic and uncomplicated. Our cutting, nagging comments can wound them deeply, especially when the disapproval builds up over time. What we think of as no more than a little jab about a specific incident becomes a stabbing wound that leaves a hole in their manhood. Yet equally as powerful are our simple, honest, even offhand compliments that can make our husbands feel like a million bucks. When we make it our business to remind them of their position in Christ and the potential and possibility that lies within them—not because we're patronizing them but because we truly believe it—they feel on top of the world. One man told me that a little compliment his wife paid him one morning as he was leaving for work caused him to have confidence in his abilities all day at the office. It pays for us to choose wisely what we say and how we choose to say it.

And . . . to *whom* we say it.

Husbands have a way of detecting the mood of conversations you're having with other women. He knows if the sentiments you express when he isn't around are complimentary or not. The talks you have with others must be carefully considered and tempered with grace, even when you rightfully need to be honest about what's going on in your home to someone who can offer you godly advice. Your husband should never be ashamed to enter a conversation you've already started or be humiliated when he runs into a woman you've been talking to. He should have confidence and trust that his wife is esteeming him to others, not laughing at him behind his back.

Again, this doesn't mean shielding him from being held accountable for weaknesses in his character or any faultiness in his thinking, especially those things that are causing dangerous harm to your marriage and family. But it does mean being sure the picture you paint of him in public is uplifting and edifying. A friend of ours once shared with me how good it feels to know that whenever he sees his wife talking and laughing with other women, like at church or at a party, he knows—because of his wife's promise to him (and his to her)—that she's not running him down to somebody else. He doesn't need to know what they're snickering about; he just knows it's not about him.

Now perhaps your husband has consistently proven that he's not worthy of your trust. He's been careless with money, drawn to addictions, perhaps even unfaithful to his marriage vows. The reason you can't ascribe high value to his character, you say, is because he hasn't shown you very much of it. And you're right—his carelessness, laziness, neglect, or lack of integrity is not your fault. You are not responsible for what he's done and is doing, even if you've been less than careful about loving him well and feeding his ego. In many cases, the wisest next step in marriages where trust has been severely broken is to seek godly, mature counsel on how to proceed in a healthy, redemptive, united way. But even you—even now—can resolve to affirm your husband and to promise that your trust in him is not gone forever. It may need to be reconstructed with the aid of outside help and ongoing accountability, but he needs to know that your heart's desire is to reestablish confidence in him.

So even in the most minor of baby steps, will you begin inching forward in your visible signs of trust and affirmation toward him? Will you allow him the new (or at least long-forgotten) experience of walking into the day with his wife's love and esteem trailing behind him? Will you look him in the eye and tell him you're not devising a plan B, a fallback arrangement in case he doesn't ultimately pan out— that *he* is your one and only plan A?

What would a man do differently if he knew he couldn't lose his wife's love and respect, no matter what he did? I don't pose this question breezily. I understand the serious implications involved. I know why you may shudder at it. But read it and ask it again. And consider . . .

Would he feel so freed from responsibility and consequence that he'd indulge his self-centeredness even more than he already does? Or—and this is likely—would the ironclad assurance of your support and devotion inspire him to greater things than he's proven capable of before, breakthroughs that would end up benefitting *both* of you with richer blessing and depth of relationship? Only one way to find out.

And now, to the second of his fears.

2. *His fear of being controlled.* We looked at the different roles of men and women in our resolution regarding biblical femininity. Males and females have equal value, but we are not the same. Your standards and opinions are different from his, perhaps in many areas of potential contention. But that doesn't mean his way is necessarily wrong. It's just different. Perhaps even right. At least worth listening to and considering. If you try to control him and force him into your way of thinking, you will break something that probably doesn't need fixing, just understanding and valuing.

When your husband feels like he's being controlled, he will eventually shut down completely, relegating his role of leadership to you, since "you seem to be doing such a good job at it anyway." The result is a shadow of the man you once knew and loved—a deflated, disinterested slacker who makes few decisions and shows little initiative. Then, in the vicious cycle created by this marital dynamic, you become increasingly overwhelmed, frustrated, and upset because you feel like you're bearing the burden *he* should be carrying—when in actuality, it's the very burden you snatched away from him because you didn't like how he was doing it.

But if, on the other hand, he doesn't feel like he's being bullied out of his God-given position as the leader in the home or held up to your overbearing, micromanaging scrutiny, he'll not only be more likely to settle in to his potential but also to seek your help and willingly relinquish certain responsibilities that you're clearly more equipped to handle. In other words, he won't mind admitting that you're better equipped than him in a particular area. When that happens, some of the things you've been vying to claim more control and influence over may come back to you without a fight—as if it was his idea all along—once he doesn't feel like he has no choice but to abdicate.

And you know what? This could also rebound to you in the areas of intimacy and romance. A man who feels controlled by his wife loses much of his desire for being tender toward a woman who sounds, acts, and treats him more like his mother. No wonder he doesn't look dreamily into her eyes or spark romantic endeavors with her the way he used to do when she just wanted to be his sweetheart and allowed him to be her champion.

I've never seen a car whose engine started just because the driver was sitting behind the wheel, demanding that it move forward. Certain things need to happen before she can get the car to go—key in the ignition, maneuvered into the right gear, gently pressing on the accelerator. Men aren't "turned on" by a demanding, screaming wife who doesn't recognize their value and significance but by wives who know the strategic steps for getting them started. Control and intimacy are on opposing, collision courses that will inevitably banish passion to the long-term parking lot, eventually rusting out, in need of major repair. Backing off your husband helps him feel more confident, more ful-filled. The result is a guy who loves being around you, enjoys long talks with you, and remembers how to romance you.

Two fears. Fear of *inadequacy* and fear of being *controlled*. You can do something about them both. In fact, your husband will never get over them without you.

But *with you* . . . who knows?

You are the "suitable" helper (Genesis 2:18 NASB) the Lord has given him to assist him in realizing that with God's help he can be

THE RESOLUTION for WOMEN

proficient, honorable, trustworthy, and fully capable of becoming the man God intends him to be despite His fears.

My friend Raina is beautiful, outgoing, energetic, and full of life. She's involved in ministry, has a great home, fun kids, and—best of all—a happy husband. Sure, they've had their struggles through the years. Financial. Health related. He hasn't always made good decisions; neither has she. But take one look at them, and you can tell— she's got a contented man.

After thirty-three years of marriage, they still hold hands. They go out on dates. He opens the car door for her. They laugh with each other and enjoy their inside jokes. I've seen him glance over at her through a crowd and give her a little wink. I've watched them leave early from a gathering or get-together so they can go home and have what they call some "real fun" alone. They've got the kind of marriage anyone would want.

When Jerry and I were out with the two of them recently, I asked Raina's husband what the key was, why he was still so happy and so obviously in love. He said it hadn't always been this way and that they still had plenty of personal struggles to contend with. But really, his explanation was simple: "She lets me be her man. When I see her relax because she's confident in my ability, showing me that she thinks I'm trustworthy, it makes me feel secure in my manhood. In this relationship, I get to be a man."

And there's nothing happier (or more attractive) than a man who actually feels like one.

So, sister, it's your husband's turn. To feel like a man.

Start with the next twenty-four hours. Just one day. Refuse to correct him, to offer any unsolicited advice, or to criticize his choices. Go to the restaurant he wants; let the kids wear the clothes he picked out for them to put on; use the driving directions he got online. I know it might take every ounce of emotional restraint available, but just keep looking out the passenger-side window and pray for God to pour in some more. And He will. He'll give you what it takes to be the kind of wife that wins her man. You may not like the food, may not like how your children are dressed, may have to circle the block ten times looking for the right address. But you will have won a great victory. Your husband won't feel belittled or drained dry by your comments, suggestions, and commands. He won't feel estranged and distant from you. You'll be on the path to winning him back by making him feel honored and respected.

And that feels good.

That's a smart girl he married.

- *Single sister, take time this week to talk with a married woman whose marriage your admire. Ask her to read this chapter and share with you the ways she's successfully combatted these twin fears in her husband's life. Then ask her to share those things that, in hindsight, she would do differently if she could. Hear her. Learn from her.*

- *What does your husband do or say that shows signs of these two fears in his life? After recording your answers, consider what you are possibly doing to contribute to them, as well as what you could do to defuse them.*

- *How does soothing a husband's fears ultimately benefit the wife?*

- *"A wise woman builds her home, but a foolish woman tears it down with her own hands" (Proverbs 14:1 NLT). What are some practical ways you can begin to "build your house"?*

- *If your friends were to describe your husband, based solely on your comments and conversations about him, what do you think their depiction would be?*

Need a Little Peace and Quiet?

Thank you for sticking with me this long. I know this book is not a beach novel. And I also know, even though we've marched bravely through some courageous subjects together, that this calling of being a wife is perhaps the tallest order of all, no matter how lovely, thoughtful, protective, and intentional your husband is.

We need help in this role. We need direction.

And like always, God's Word is the best place to get it.

Admittedly, when we open the Bible looking for specific ways to handle personal situations in our marriage, we may not always find the answers spelled out with step-by-step clarity. That's a job for the Holy Spirit, communicating to us through an ongoing dialogue of Scripture and the wise help of godly people He's equipped to walk with us through these types of difficulties.

But the Word does contain big-picture truths that are always instructive—direction that applies to all of us, in every case. Peter's first letter is one place where we get a huge hint at what loving and honoring our husbands is supposed to look like:

Wives . . . be submissive to your husbands so that, if any of them do not believe the word, they may be won over without words by the behavior of their wives, when they see the purity and reverence of

your lives. Your beauty should not come from outward adornment,
such as braided hair and the wearing of gold jewelry and fine
clothes. Instead, it should be that of your inner self, the unfading
beauty of a gentle and quiet spirit, which is of great worth in
God's sight. For this is the way the holy women of the past who
put their hope in God used to make themselves beautiful. They
were submissive to their own husbands. (1 Peter 3:1–5 NIV)

You know, it's easy to skip over Scripture passages when they appear excerpted in a book like this, so be sure not to let that happen. Read back over these choice words of God slowly and deliberately. Go ahead, I'll wait . . .

Now I have to be honest with you. These verses have upset me once or twice in my life. Reading this description conjures up pictures of a woman from *Little House on the Prairie* days, with her never-before-cut hair coiled up in a bun on top of her head, her ankle-length skirt hoisted over a thick, rustly petticoat. Nothing wrong with that. It's just not me. And I thought it unfair of God to expect me to fill that role. "Gentle and quiet"? I'm a gregarious, boisterous extrovert. Can my husband's heart only be won by a personality type God didn't see fit to suit me with?

And yet this is God's Word we're dealing with. So obviously He is trying to tell me something important, something I need to understand. And if you—like me—are a believer in Christ, with God's Spirit dwelling within you, then He can be trusted to empower us to do this, enabling us to accomplish something we cannot do with our on-hand, natural resources.

Like being "gentle and quiet"—key ingredients to a happy marriage.

Gentle. In the Greek language of the Bible, this is the word *praus*, meaning not to be overly impressed with oneself, to be humble, considerate, and meek. Simply put, we're being asked to become a soft place for our husbands to land amid the hard world in which we all live. To be kind—the same way we want them to be kind to us.

Can you resolve to do that? Can you stop and think before you blurt out another criticism? If not, would you be so kind as to keep your inconsiderate opinion to yourself and ask God to give you nicer things to say?

Don't just think of it as biting your tongue, however. What are some ways you could proactively express kindness toward your spouse? Is there something you could do for him that would show your desire to think of his needs above your own? He may not ask for it. He may not expect it. He may not even deserve it in your opinion. But what a difference it could make.

Perhaps you already make a habit of doing these types of things. Good. You should be applauded for that. But let me ask you a question I often ask myself: Do some of these ways you try to show him kindness mean more to you than they do to him?

Maybe you could make a point of watching him over the next week to find out what he really likes—little things you may have overlooked—and determine how you could insert little changes into your routine that would speak kindness to him in those areas. If you made it your business to study him and really know him well, would you find some better ways—ways that matter to him—to express your kindness? This kind of intentionality would show you're serious about being "gentle."

For example, for the first fifteen years of our marriage, I didn't drink coffee (and never had), so I never really put much thought into how to fix a cup for my husband "just the way he likes it." But taking time to learn Jerry's coffee preferences has meant a lot to him. It shows him that I care, that I'm thinking about him. Simple, yet powerful. It makes him feel prioritized and significant to me, and the ripple effect of that feeling ultimately benefits me and our marriage.

Another example comes from knowing that your husband feels affirmed when you are enthusiastically intimate with him. In her book *For Women Only*, researcher Shaunti Feldhahn reports that 97 percent of men say they want to feel desired and sought out by their wives, not simply tolerated when they want to have sex.[3] Most likely your husband is one of these men. A wife that is proactive—initiating intimacy in the bedroom—causes her husband to feel loved, respected, admired, and treasured.

Admittedly, this can be quite a challenge when emotional connection between the two of you is low or when your physical needs have changed with the seasons of life or even just with age. And yet, even the smallest gesture and engagement toward intimacy with your husband bolsters confidence deeply in his soul.

So carefully consider your man. How can you proactively communicate kindness to him? Not just peace but . . .

Quiet. Again, of course, it comes from a Greek word—*hesychois.* And much to my delight, it doesn't mean to be silent, never uttering a word or offering an opinion. It means to be well-ordered, to lead a peaceable and discreet life, thus lightening the task of the other person in the relationship. That last part is what really hits home—*lightening the load of your husband.*

If we will funnel our wifely behavior and responses through this biblical filter, we will intentionally become more careful and circumspect. We'll try hard to see things from our husband's perspective without just running roughshod over him with our own stances, viewpoints, and interpretations. We'll keep the larger, longer-term goals of our marriage in mind instead of getting bogged down in little nitpicking skirmishes over nothing. Rather than fighting to keep ourselves from being overlooked or taken advantage of, we'll focus on what would help him complete his tasks for our family with more wisdom, vision, and clear thinking. We'll attempt to make things easier instead of harder for him, tempering our words and actions with peace and discreetness, causing him to feel more confident because he knows we're not here to tear him down but to build him up.

Single sister, this is how you must approach marriage—asking yourself how you can be a "load lifter" and a "burden lightener" instead of a needy woman looking to be served, coddled, and made content by her man.

That's some pretty tough talk, and you might give yourself a pass to skip over it if you thought I'd made all of this up. But I didn't. It's the ageless, venerated truth from God's own Word.

And it's worth it. Because in the end these two powerful words—"gentle" and "quiet"—go together to spell something that keeps us looking attractive to our men long after our outward appearance has lost much of its sheen and sparkle. Peter calls it "unfading beauty," as opposed to "outward adornment." It's something your husband will still be intrigued by and interested in for years to come.

My mom used to tell me about this—this feminine mystery—before I really had a true appreciation for it. I couldn't quite understand how a woman could maintain any type of mystique to a man she'd been living with for so long, sharing the ins and outs of daily life. But she knew something I'm only beginning to learn. What's really alluring to a husband of ten, twenty, thirty, forty, fifty years is the "unfading beauty of a gentle and quiet spirit." That's the deep treasure that keeps the intrigue burning and passionate.

According to Peter, this type of lifestyle has enough power to transform a husband's eternal destiny, to win him over to Christ without our having to say a word, just by noticing the way we operate. If these behaviors of ours have the capability of doing *that*, then surely they're strong enough to deal with the day-to-day issues that can cause our marriages such grief.

There's real power in gentleness and quietness.

So despite my original belief, this is not some antiquated suggestion only fit for those who haven't yet advanced into modern society. It's for everybody—even for stylish, contemporary, high-heel wearing, technology using, capable, Spirit-filled women who want their husbands fulfilled by the honor we give them.

It's for you. It's for me.

And done well, it's an honor.

- *Single woman, if marriage is something you desire, making this resolution even now—before you say "I do"—can change the trajectory of your life. So consider it carefully in light of your current perspective on what it means to become a wife. Commit to seeking*

the wise counsel and advice of other women whose marriages you admire, and prayerfully weigh their insights as you determine when and if marriage is right for you, and whether a particular man you're currently dating or have in mind is the one you want to join your life with.

- Married woman, begin this resolution by asking your husband what honor looks like to him. What causes him to be dishonored? You may be surprised by his answer. Creatively consider one thing you can do to be proactively kind. Then with a prayerful, honest, hopeful heart, sign this resolution into practice. Prepare to live it for the good of your marriage and the glory of Christ.

❧ HONORING MY HUSBAND ☙

I will be faithful to my husband and honor him in my conduct and conversation in order to bring glory to the name of the Lord. I will aspire to be a suitable partner for him to help him reach his God-given potential.

_____

LOVING MY
CHILDREN

*A resolution to train my kids in
righteousness*

True Love

I want to have babies again.

At least that's the way I feel when I scroll through my social media feed. Somehow the wonders of algorithm technology have zeroed in on my tendency to drool over cute baby faces, captured with all their giggles and oops and stumbles and messes. My search feature is always inundated with a surplus of cuteness, with little kids dressed in well-imagined, delicately placed outfits surrounded by poetic, photo-worthy scenes. It makes my heart skip a couple of beats and translates me back nearly two decades to a time when our own boys folded deftly into my arms. I think of the play dates, of all those quiet, cooing moments in the dim light of their toddler bedrooms. I remember those precious times with a fondness I can nearly taste.

And, for a little while, I want to do it all over again.

Then I turn off my phone and snap back to reality—the reality I've lived (and am still living), the one that reminds me what raising kids is actually like. All the cute images and videos in the world don't tell the whole story of what a woman quickly realizes once she's given birth or has adopted, once her life is gloriously upended for the foreseeable future, sweeping her into the throes of real-life, everyday motherhood.

Soon that little child's personality begins to unfold, and a mother begins to grasp the full charge she's been given, the solemn responsibility of her role here. Her main priority, though sweetly interrupted at times by rollicking belly laughs and shared Oreos, is to shepherd this beautiful human into adulthood. To enjoy those bits and pieces while remaining clear on the time-consuming, all-encompassing, often emotionally draining investment of herself in the shaping and steering of a young life.

This is the part that will require her dogged commitment, which might just keep her too tied up to craft Instagram-worthy photos on a regular basis. Instead she'll be busy doing her number-one job: leading her children with diligent intentionality, instilling them with strong moral fiber, guiding them toward becoming men and women filled with integrity, girded with responsibility, and firmly rooted in a love for and honor of God.

I can certainly attest to being caught off guard by this reality, then having to give myself grace and adjust my expectations through each season of motherhood. Right from the beginning, becoming a mom was a thunderous shock to my normally independent, spontaneous nature. With the birth of our first son, I found myself hardly prepared for the discipline of being organized and keeping a schedule—necessary endeavors for any mom who hopes to retain some sense of sanity. Suddenly my life was no longer my own. My needs didn't come first anymore. Someone else's interests now pulled the primary spot.

And that was just with *one* child.

When I had my second son nineteen months later, followed by our (surprise!) third son four years after that, I became more and more aware of the incredible mixture of responsibility and privilege involved in raising these boys. In the midst of long, tiring days and frequently even longer nights, my perspective began to change. I started seeing my efforts through the lens of eternal ramifications. These little men, after all—even though they're not such little men any longer—are still my chief way of reproducing God's image on earth, proliferating the agenda of the Father Himself through these once little human beings who will hopefully become leaders of their own homes and in society one day.

So while there's nothing wrong (and everything right) with playing on the floor and making homemade waffles and posting digital images of our children's first haircuts, we must remember that our principal charge and mission as parents is to send our boys and girls into the world as young people who bear God's Spirit, who are purposeful about His mission for their lives, and who are intent on being His agent for change on the planet. They are like "arrows . . . in the hand of a mighty man" (Psalm 127:4 kjv)—sharpened, directed, and sent forth into the world to accomplish the tasks for which they were divinely created. This is your resolution as the mother. And it won't just happen on its own.

But other things will.

Since children's normal proclivity leans in the direction of their fleshly tendencies (just like ours), it doesn't take much for them to learn selfishness, to indulge in rebellion, and to get sucked into the vacuum of disrespect and disregard for others. Left to their own devices, and to the electronic devices that can so easily consume their time and attention, they will inevitably succumb to the subtle (and not so subtle) thrusts of a culture that applauds these tendencies and can shift their moral compasses. But get this. Are you ready?

Get. This.

You and I are the mechanisms God has put in place to keep today's corrupting systems of thought from taking firm root and then taking full effect in the hearts of our children. You are in position to intervene. You, sister, have been placed specifically in your children's lives to make them rebels—nonconformists who don't meld seamlessly into a culture that's encouraging them to rebel against you.

Will this be easy? Not on your life.

Will your investment yield a perfect result? Not on your life.

And yet we can still resolve to bring our full, Holy Spirit-empowered commitment to these tasks and then entrust the results to Him.

No matter how challenging you may find or have found this endeavor to be—no matter how discouraged this resolution may cause you to feel or how many years you think you've already wasted—now is a good time to start with your toddlers or teenagers, your adult children or your grandchildren, becoming in their lives what God has placed you in this position to be. It won't be without difficulty, but it *will* be worth it—not only for the benefit of the kids you love so much but because you'll be fulfilling one of the purposes for which you were created: to be the key influencer of these children, these precious ones God has always known He'd be giving you. If you have them, parenting them in this way is among your highest, most primary callings.

And even if you're reading this before becoming a mother—even if God may choose in His wise, good, and sovereign plan to bestow you with *other* blessings besides the experience of motherhood—there are still some valuable things to learn as a friend, a counselor, and a role model in the lives of other children.

As with our last resolution, the topic of parenting is so all-consuming, we could read volumes on it and still be left with much that can only be learned through personal experience. So I've purposefully titled this resolution "Loving My Children" in order to narrow down our focus to this one particular theme.

Love.

How can this best be seen in a parent-child relationship?

Scripture teaches us that love is not passive; it is demonstrative and active. "Let us not love in word or speech, but in action and in truth" (1 John 3:18). So the first thing to know is that love in a biblical, godly sense is expressed through *visible actions*. Second, it's intended to serve the best interests of another by instilling and encouraging in them the practical experience of *living in God's truth*.

When our primary goal as mothers is teaching our children God's truth, the whole focus of our parenting changes. We begin to filter every decision we make through the question, "Is this in my children's best interest, and will it help them grow into adults who know God's truth and desire to live according to it?"

The outworkings of this resolution may not always sound like love to your children. To them, *love* means being given permission to peruse endless hours of YouTube, digest inordinate amounts of ice cream, spend their whole allowance (again) on Amazon, and be relieved of most (if not all) responsibility around the house and to the family. In their shortsightedness they're unable to see and understand what their "best interests" are, beyond a specific moment of enjoyment. So a fair share of your "actions" toward them will not always translate as *love* to their minds. They may think your so-called love is overbearing and unnecessarily restrictive.

And in all honesty, loving your kids in the way we've defined it here will often not even feel like love to *you*. There will be times when your requirement to be loving will go against your natural inclination that longs to coddle and caress these sweet little angels whose diapers you once changed in the glow of the morning sun. Sometimes the greatest enemy to loving our kids is . . . us. We so easily allow our feelings to guide us instead of making the tough, resilient decision to love our children with wisdom, maturity, discernment, and discipline.

If we're going to love them as defined by Scripture, we cannot ultimately aspire to their friendship. We're their parents. And there's a difference in those roles. Hopefully one day these two things will dovetail, but today we are in the position to teach our kids how to live in a way pleasing to God, a way that leads them toward becoming respectful, responsible adults. Yes, ask the Lord to bless you with their friendship, but this cannot be your primary pursuit now.

So don't take this resolution lightly. Ask yourself, "Does the way I'm raising my son or daughter reveal that I'm a 'loving' mom, or just a mom 'in love' with my child—a pushover who's easily swayed by their tears, tantrums, and ever-changing mood swings?" If there's rarely anything you do that doesn't *feel* like love—to *them*—then you may have cause to wonder. If they like everything you do and the way you do it, you may be a mom *in love* with your child who needs to work on being truly *loving*.

Because love is not child's play. It's serious business.

And our children need parents who are on the job.

- *In light of a decision you are currently facing with your child, what would differentiate a "loving" response from an "in love" one?*

- *In all honesty, which do you desire more . . .*
    - to be your child's friend?
    - to be your child's parent?

- *How does this affect the way you parent?*

- *If you are not a parent, consider your own upbringing. If your parents were overly indulgent, how did this affect you? What if they were too strict?*

The Soul Shaper

The *Soul Shaper*.
The *Intentional Encourager*.
The *Discipline Dealer*.

These three roles represent some of the key functions of motherhood. As we explore each one in the next few chapters, I want you to remember that your unique family dynamic will impact the way you express these roles in your mothering. What I will paint in these pages is not an ideal to shoot for, but only a tool to help calibrate your parenting compass. The point is not to be flawless in executing the details or to try precisely mirroring what other people (including your own parents) have done. Your family and your children are unique. And as your children grow through different stages and your family dynamics adjust into next year's version of normal, I can tell you from personal experience that you should expect these roles to shift as your children get older.

So as you read, relax. And ask the Holy Spirit how He wants to use these insights to help you in this season of your life.

Let's consider the soul shaper first.

Ah, the human soul. A magnificent composite of mind, will, and emotions, as well as the seat of the conscience. Every person is created by God with this part of their makeup in place. The only problem—and it's a big one—is that without the indwelling presence of God's

216

Spirit, the soul is completely degenerate, ruled by fleshly lusts and totally separated from God.

In this state, conscience alone is unable to make accurate judgments concerning right and wrong, which leads the individual to live in a way that is displeasing to God. He can't help it. None of us can. We come into life with souls that are in desperate need of being awakened and reprogrammed.

And only a personal relationship with Jesus Christ can do it. He is the one and only hope for a lost soul.

Including your child's soul.

Yeah, I hate to break it to you like this, if you weren't aware of it, but . . . your child arrived to you spiritually lost. As sweet and beautiful as our kids are, they are each born as sinners in need of being rescued from themselves. And just like us—just like everybody—Christ is the only One who can do anything about it. He alone can . . .

- keep their unruly *minds* from becoming the enemy's stomping grounds.
- bend their *will* until it wants to follow God's ambitions for them.
- steady their runaway *emotions* before they get our kids into all kinds of trouble.
- awaken their deadened *conscience* so it can be led by God's Spirit when you're not around to tell them the difference between right and wrong.

And because they need Jesus so desperately, you are the one who must consistently ask the Lord to stir a desire for Him in their hearts, even from birth. You are the one who keeps praying this prayer even when they grow up and leave your home. You are the one who has "no greater joy than this: to hear that my children are walking in truth" (3 John 4).

This makes you . . . a *soul shaper*.

The soul shaper is stunningly aware that her prayers for her child are significant and that once her child receives salvation, she is God's primary tool to work alongside the Holy Spirit to see that the transforming process occurs effectively in her child's soul. Whether she is married or raising her children alone, she knows she cannot accomplish this by herself, so she involves other entities like her church and relatives to assist in the effort. But she and (if she's married) her husband know that the main responsibility is theirs. They don't allow anyone else to take their place as the primary influencers in their children's lives. Helping them know and become sensitive to God's conviction, teaching them how to recognize His way of directing them through their conscience—these are things the soul shaper helps her kids discover little by little, day by day.

And as her children mature, she continues to work along with God's Spirit to see that this shaping takes place. She doesn't make her child-rearing decisions in reaction to their tears and tantrums but expresses her love by determining ahead of time what will best complement God's work in the shaping of their minds, will, emotions, and consciences. She sees herself as a partner with God in His work, helping to steward His transforming process in their lives. So she trains them by clearly defining and demonstrating expectations, practicing these directives into habits, and then executing consequences when her loving rules are rejected.

Even later in life, when she's no longer surrounded by little noses, toes, and voices, she still sees herself as God's partner in this effort, asking Him continually to clarify how she can be used for His purposes in her grown children's lives. She knows that her work is never really done.

Tall orders, huh?

And yet as a mother truly resolved to love her kids, the soul shaper can do no less. She considers herself a warrior, fighting for her family throughout her entire lifetime. She's not willing to sit idly by while other people and cultural paradigms tamper with her children's mind-sets, disrupting the soul's transformation. She knows that if their minds are ever to think and operate in a way that's pleasing to the Father, they must hear and see much more of God's righteousness than they do of the world's filth. So she carefully, vigilantly considers how to make sure that one outweighs the other, monitoring the kinds of influences she allows to affect their lives.

This is her life's work, and she protects her investment at all costs. She refuses to allow the pollutants of mindless entertainment, vile suggestions, and godless teaching to take center stage in her children's psyche. While she realizes that she cannot completely shield her children from everything, she does her best to counterbalance it with a steady stream of goodness—those things that are true, honest, just, pure, lovely, and full of virtue (Philippians 4:8).

She doesn't take the night off by sending her "life's work" into environments that make her uneasy, even if it's more convenient to do so, or letting them participate in an event where she's not clear on the kind of activities or supervision that's offered. She is concerned about *every* aspect of her children's lives, and she takes this role with the utmost seriousness.

She's not a perfect parent; she's just a woman who believes that her parenting is kingdom business.

Additionally, the soul shaper isn't always on defense. She works proactively to stand against her children's natural, human tendencies and the world's continued influence. That's why she resolves to be a woman of the Word. She knows the importance of saturating her children in the Scriptures, and she is creative and consistent in making this happen. She is keenly aware that knowing and learning the Word are not only paramount in helping her succeed as a mother but in helping her children find success in life as well.

So she diligently and deliberately reads the Bible to them. She requires them to tuck God's Word away in their hearts when they are young (Psalm 119:10–11), and even if her kids hate this process as much as they hate doing their daily homework, she doesn't let up. Doesn't let a little moaning, groaning, and pouting discourage her from maintaining her leading role in shaping souls. She knows this steady discipline will cause their minds to be transformed, their spirits renewed, their ears more easily opened to the Spirit's voice as they grow into adulthood.

This leads her to post Scripture verses throughout the house, where her kids will pass by them on the way to brushing their teeth or getting an apple from the fruit basket. She wafts the Word through the air with worship music while she's cooking and cleaning and catching up on the laundry. She gathers with other believers in the context of her local Bible-teaching church so her children can see that her family is not alone and strange to believe this stuff but is part of a whole family called the body of Christ.

She is kind and tender, but in this—in her soul shaping—she is radical and vigilant.

Her stance is strong, her resolve sure.

She is a soul shaper—on mission to use these few, short years she has with her children to help them conform into the image of Christ.

Oh, and one more thing. The soul shaper knows that she will never have the strength to persist in this endeavor if she herself is not on the same journey of transformation that she's working so diligently to cultivate in her children. If they are ever to know God (not just know *about* Him), she must be a woman who expresses His joy, loves His Word, is honest about her shortcomings and her need for grace, and enjoys His company as much as she tells them *they* should. She doesn't pound the "thou shalt nots" into their heads as much as she shows them through her smile and lifestyle how much fun this adventure with God can be. She realizes that nothing can speed her children's spiritual growth faster than when they see the proof of it in her own eyes. So she follows the clear pattern of Deuteronomy 6:5–7, nurturing her own relationship with God first, and then systematically surrounding her children with evidence of His truth.

[You will] love the LORD your God with all your heart, with all your soul, and with all your strength. These words that I am giving you today are to be in your heart. Repeat them to your children. Talk about them when you sit in your house and when you walk along the road, when you lie down and when you get up.

This is the soul shaper's inspiration, resolving that from this day forward, and with God's abundant help, she will guard the spiritual thermostat setting in her home. Because that's how a mother loves her children well.

And you can do it.

We can do it.

A transformed child starts with a transformed mom. And she—I mean you, the soul shaper—lives to make sure this transformation happens.

- *What are some ways the soul shaper partners with God defensively? Proactively?*

- *This question is for everyone, but single mom, you especially: Who are some people who can help walk alongside you in this highly challenging resolution?*

- *How can you creatively live your Christian life openly before your children?*

- *If you are married and your husband is not resolved to take the helm of spiritual leadership in your home, do not be discouraged and allow your children's spiritual health to flounder. Lead your children in devotions and prayer. Encourage them in Scripture memory, and speak God's truth over their lives and identity.*

- *As your children get older, their schedules busier, and their attention more diverse and divided, the way you implement this resolution will undoubtedly need to shift. Don't be afraid to reevaluate the current realities of your evolving family and ask the Lord to help you relax into it. Then trust His Spirit to show you creative ways to continue moving toward your family goals. No effort is too small or insignificant. Trust Him to multiply your investment.*

The Intentional Encourager

It's a classic Bible story. God appears to King Solomon one night and tells him He'll give him anything he wants. Just name it. But instead of asking for health and wealth or prosperity and prestige, Solomon surprisingly asks for *wisdom*, a request that meets not only with God's favor but also with the promise of more "riches, wealth, and glory" than any king before him or any king yet to come would ever experience (2 Chronicles 1:7–12).

I'm amazed not only by Solomon's request but with this fact: when he was presented with this incredible offer, he was only twenty years old.

Two-zero.

I ask you: What twenty-year-old do you know who, if given the kind of independence young King Solomon had, would've handled this divine opportunity in so mature and farsighted a way? Not many?

Me neither.

All I can figure is, apart from the clear hand of God moving in this young man's life, it must have had something to do with the way Solomon was raised.

His father, King David, was the most respected man in all of Israel, a person uniquely blessed by God and honored by the people for his outstanding courage and leadership. He wasn't perfect. Not by a long shot. He made some colossal mistakes in both his personal life and his parenting. But in order to rear such a sensible young man as Solomon who could respond to God's offer so carefully, so wisely, David must have done some things right, as well.

Maybe we get a clue during one of the last occasions when we hear David speaking about his son. Standing in the presence of a vast assembly of people (including, most likely, Solomon himself), David announced plans for Solomon to succeed him as king and how he intended to make preparations for him. He said . . .

> *My son Solomon—God has chosen him alone—is young*
> *and inexperienced. (1 Chronicles 29:1)*

It sounds strangely like a modern-day parent saying to his mouthy, know-it-all teenager, "Listen, buddy, you don't know *everything!*" David was open and honest about his son's deficiencies, almost in a way that sounds like a public slam or rebuke. So why did this not deflate Solomon's spirit? Why did hearing his father call him out for his youth and inexperience not make him feel condemned and worthless? Why did it just make him all the more eager and enthusiastic to become the wisest king he could be?

I think some of it had to do with that middle phrase his father spoke just as boldly as the last: "God has chosen him alone." Even with Solomon's obvious weaknesses, David affirmed what he saw the Lord doing in his life, not just in private but before a vast gathering of people. He was telling them plainly the plans and preparation he was making right then for the future tasks his son would undertake. He even encouraged them—despite his son's failings—to assist in providing large amounts of treasure and building materials for the temple that Solomon would one day build. David was calling his son to great things and enlisting others to help. He was supporting him at great sacrifice and proving that he had confidence in what his boy was capable of doing and becoming, despite the current immaturities.

In other words, *David believed in his son*. And it made Solomon want to live up to that expectation. He didn't have any problem with his dad's being honest—about his inexperience and all—because David peppered that sentiment with a father's encouragement. As a result, he raised a child sensible and shrewd enough to ask the Lord for wisdom above every other delectable option on the table.

David's example teaches us something powerful. To raise children who are wise, focused, discerning, and passionate about the things that really matter in life, you and I need to be *intentional encouragers*. Like David. Even when Solomon's gifts couldn't yet be clearly seen, even when his talents had yet to be honed, even when his leadership skills were not yet intact, David encouraged Solomon to see the potential in himself—and encouraged others to see it in him too. Instead of belittling or discouraging his son, David seemed to accept the normalcy of this season in Solomon's life. Sure, he was just a kid, prone to making the immature mistakes of the inexperienced. But his father saw a king in him and told everyone to prepare for his becoming one even though his current choices and actions might seem contrary to the notion.

That's the role of the intentional encourager.

And that's you.

The intentional encourager is honest with her kids. She tells them what they need to hear, even when it's not what they *want* to hear. She doesn't overlook their immaturity, mistakes, and mishaps; but when she brings these points up, she doesn't do it with an air of disapproval and low expectation. She chooses rather to temper her honesty with the grace of edification and encouragement. She goes to great lengths to protect her children's spirits by making sure the overarching tone of their relationship is one of approval. She doesn't try to force her children to be more like somebody else—especially more like one of their siblings. Even during those seasons of their individual lives that she wishes would hurry along more quickly than others, she resists the urge to compare one's progress with another. She seeks rather to focus on the unique gifts, talents, and skills God is patiently perfecting in that particular child, doing everything possible to foster it, even when it's different from what she expected or is developing more slowly than she'd hoped.

She just knows God has purposes "prepared" for her children to "walk in" (Ephesians 2:10), and He has consecrated each kid—set them apart—to accomplish those God-given purposes.

Eventually.

And so she fights not to become discouraged during those periods of glaring immaturity and inexperience. She encourages herself (and intentionally surrounds herself with others who do the same) so that she won't become deflated, not wallowing in those inner voices that say she's a terrible mother. Instead she tries to relax during this current stage of her kids' lives, reminding herself (as well as others who may be starting to doubt it) that her children have been chosen by God for specific purposes. She sees destiny in them even when they're "young and inexperienced" and does everything she can to edify and encourage those traits that make them special while applying appropriate guidance and correction. Even when staring their failures in the face, she remains vigilant and takes the necessary steps to get them back on track. She never stops believing that her diligent work as a mother now will provide the framework for her children's success later.

She's an encourager—an *intentional* encourager—who expresses love to her children by not allowing them to settle for immaturity or succumb to mediocrity. She inspires excellence not by demanding that they meet the arbitrary standards of others but that they rise to the achievable challenge of their God-given purpose and potential in every arena of life. She speaks highly of her children to others and is not bashful about soliciting positive, prayerful help in calling out the best in her kids. She is their most honest confidant and also their biggest cheerleader.

Like David, she believes in her children.

And who knows? This kind of intentional encouragement might cause a twenty-year-old child of yours, like Solomon, who might otherwise be permanently swayed into lifestyles, habits, or inappropriate attachments, to turn his or her face toward the heavens and say, "Lord, give me wisdom."

When they do, you can count on God to grant them what they ask. And more.

- *Record some of the unique characteristics of each of your children. How can you call these out for specific encouragement?*

- *List some of the immature actions and temperaments in them that might normally discourage you. Keep this list in a place where you can always be reminded to pray regarding them, and consider who you can enlist to encourage your child in these areas.*

- *Carefully consider how you can make the overarching tone of your relationship with your child one of encouragement and approval.*

The Discipline Dealer

Years ago, when our sons were still teething and potty training, Jerry and I met a successful businessman in his mid-forties who'd been married for twenty years and had two teenage sons. Sitting in his office, listening to Bill talk about his family, was captivating to me. He and his wife had an immensely enjoyable relationship with their boys, a fun-loving connection that made spending time together as a family the high points of their week.

Did you hear that? Their teenagers *wanted* to spend time with them, and they *wanted* to spend time with their teenagers.

Intrigued by this all-too-rare relationship between parents and their teenagers, I asked Bill what he attributed it to. His answer was simple yet profound: "We enjoy them so much now because we were serious about training and instilling discipline in them when they were younger. We envisioned what kind of adults we wanted them to be, then we trained them accordingly while they were little and insisted that they comply with those expectations. It wasn't easy, but it's been worth it."

He went on to recount how guests who visited in their home had always been stunned at the boys' willingness to set the table before dinner or assist their mom in getting the laundry gathered from all the hampers on washing day without complaining. The respect with which these brothers spoke, not only to other adults but also to each other, clearly demonstrated the deeply ingrained regard for others that existed in their home. The trust they'd earned from their parents had long remained intact because they'd been taught from the ground up the importance of being responsible.

None of this was to suggest they were a perfect family with perfect children. Bill also talked about the hard parts they'd been through— the stops and starts, the long nights and bad attitudes, the tense arguments and tough conversations. He was real with us about how hard it had been to remain consistent in their choices. But there was no doubt these parents had taken their responsibility seriously. Their sons had been purposefully, deliberately molded by caring soul shapers.

Loving parents.

The memory of that conversation has informed many of my parenting choices over the last decade, though I think even Bill would agree that intentional parenting is no guarantee of outcomes. I know mothers who seemingly did all the right things but didn't have the same results. I've seen, heard, and felt the devastating heartbreak of women who've invested everything they've known to do into their children's lives, giving it their very best, only to reel from the life choices their sons or daughters have made as they've gotten older.

A child who once quoted the verses, attended the youth group, and lived with a tender and open heart toward God is now questioning their faith, redefining their identity, or reorienting their moral compass away from biblical guidelines and perspectives. Their ears are closed to wise counsel, their heart hardened to the conviction of the Spirit, and their daily choices marked more by the culture than the influence of Christ.

I know our best efforts are only that: *best efforts* in honoring God and raising our children well. The outcome must be left in the hands of our faithful Father who loves our children even more than we do. He truly does.

Yet among the most consistent things you see in parents who raise well-adjusted children who grow into conscientious, honorable adults is this:

They are discipline dealers.

We need to be *discipline dealers*.

These are parents, like Bill and his wife, who established goals right from the start about the type of adults they wanted to see their children mature into, then put a specific plan of action in place to attain it. They never considered their children too young, cute, and irresistible to start early with implementing the discipline and training this process would entail.

As loving discipline dealers, they've been careful, of course, not to "provoke [their] children to anger" with inappropriate forms of correction, but they've been seriously hands-on about bringing them up "in the discipline and instruction of the Lord" (Ephesians 6:4 NASB). They know that *self-discipline* is only produced as the result of being lovingly *disciplined*. So they've established clear expectations and then created an environment in which their children know the boundaries and ground rules, know how to live inside them, and know what will happen if they don't comply—the immediate reinforcement of consistent, age-appropriate consequences. These parents don't threaten consequences and then fail to carry them out. Their standards are clear and dependable.

That's love.

I remember reading a book, before I had kids, that talked about how even one-year-olds are able to respond to expectations. I remember thinking how unreasonable it seemed to expect so much from a young toddler. But I also remember being surprised a few years later when my eighteen-month-old son actually *did* start saying "please" and "thank you" and picking up his own toys and putting his sippy cup in the sink instead of leaving it on the kitchen table. When I showed him what to do and spent some time training him how to do it, and corrected him when he didn't, I couldn't believe it—even little ones can learn how to behave, based on what they're taught and what they see exemplified. I haven't done it perfectly, but I am still trying to do it purposefully.

It just makes sense, doesn't it? We can't expect our children to become what we don't train them to be and reinforce in their lives.

And what goes for manners and sippy cups applies to larger life lessons as well.

If we want them to be responsible, we must train them to be responsible with their chores, homework, and personal duties, and with consequences—like loss of privileges—that result when they don't follow through. *If we want them to be considerate*, we must enforce the manners we expect them to use with siblings and friends. *If we want them to respect and submit to authority*, we must make it start with how they treat us as their parents, while also letting them see us demonstrate this same principle ourselves in our home, our work, our church life, and other areas.

The discipline dealer creates a mission statement for her children that she keeps at the forefront of her mind as she rears them. If boys, her statement might include a focus not only on responsibility and consideration of others but also on learning how to show respect for women, preparing her sons to fill well their future role as husbands, providers, and protectors. If girls, her statement might address such themes as strength, values, excellence, and initiative, as well as fostering in them an appreciation for modesty. Based on these statements, the discipline dealer can carefully, methodically spend these years doing what is required for these practices to become a regular routine in her children's lives.

One couple we know, who are raising five children, included in their mission statement a deep desire to teach their kids to honor others by encouraging them to go beyond their normal standards of doing kind things for one another. In order to accomplish this, they frequently ask their children how they can strategically honor one of their siblings—perhaps by making their bed for them, or cleaning away their plate from the table instead of just taking their own.

They're also intent on teaching responsibility. So these discipline dealers resist the naturally parental urge to repeatedly rescue or resolve every little problem their children are facing. When someone forgets to take his lunch with him, Mom doesn't automatically race to the school with sack in hand. When someone lets a homework deadline slip up on her, Mom and Dad clearly remind but sometimes allow the child to suffer the consequences of waiting till the last minute. If the kids break a window after being specifically told not to play with that ball in the house, they can expect to pay for at least a portion of the repair with their own money. These parents want their children to know that many of the things they enjoy simply as a result of being their children are not rights but privileges. And in order to maintain them, they must learn not to take them for granted. If they do, they lose the privilege.

There are discipline dealers—intent on seeing their mission of raising responsible, considerate, respectful young men and women come to fruition.

One single mom, who just sent her oldest daughter off to college, is a pro at creative, consistent, discipline dealing. When her teenager wasn't doing a good job keeping her room clean—and had the nerve to claim that this was her prerogative since the room was "hers"—Mom took the bedroom door off the hinges. So much for that "right" of privacy a teenage girl reveres! It was the worst possible punishment her daughter could imagine. But it got her to clean her room. And it made her take a big step in the direction this mother envisioned for her as a growing adult—respectful, grateful, and responsible.

Yes, being a discipline dealer requires time and effort. It will often be inconvenient and uncomfortable and a temporary blow to your reputation around the house. But the discipline dealer is willing to do it because her priority is to rear children who are responsible, respectful, compassionate, considerate, humble, selfless, generous, and gracious. People who are a joy to be around. It's ultimately the best way—the only true way—to win the hearts of your children.

- *When you sign your name to this resolution, don't feel burdened to be perfect. Rather, resolve to express biblical love to your children, and then consider this a starting point on that journey. Craft a mission statement for your children, and then implement small things that will point them in that direction. This is a resolve to see in your children the*

potential for true spiritual greatness and to care enough to give them what they need to achieve it. To love them. To really, really love them.

❧ LOVING MY CHILDREN ❧

I will demonstrate to my children how to love God with all their hearts, minds, and strength, and will train them to respect authority and live responsibly.

———————————————

LIVING WITH GRACE

A resolution to make myself and my surroundings a welcome place to be

Off Broadway

You've had the roles handpicked and the script written for a long time now. Each scene has been carefully calculated and, in your own mind, strategically rehearsed. You're certain this theatrical masterpiece will be loved by everyone involved.

After all, it was written for their own good. Their own benefit.

So you go over and over and over it again, playing your own role and then filling in the gaps for everyone else—quoting what they're supposed to say, the expressions they're supposed to use, the intonation they're supposed to reflect, the reactions they're supposed to give. Every actor has been allotted and accounted for as you exit the dressing room of your own bedroom each morning, clutching in your hand the high standards and detailed expectations for the players on the stage of your life.

There's only one problem with this production.

No one other than you even knows that it exists.

The other actors never signed up to participate. They are unknowingly existing in a role they never agreed to play and didn't realize they were expected to fill. But now the people who make up the regular cast of your life—husband, daughter, son, friend, sibling, parent—are enslaved by your expectations, held captive to roles you wrote for them without their consent. They'd like to be themselves, to experience the same freedom they find in other places, around other people. But here at home, here with you, going out of character can cost them dearly.

The crushed look on your face.

The stunned rejection in your response.

The disapproval dripping from your voice.

It's clear you'll not stand for anyone messing with this production, this script, this play of yours. And so they don't. They play along. They have to. You'll have it no other way. But in the process, they lose themselves. They forget who they really are. They learn to live without their freedom. Their authenticity. Ultimately without their joy.

They just do your bidding. It's easier that way.

But this production ends today, as we resolve to be women of grace.

This woman recognizes and admits that, yes, she has a predetermined plot line for her life and surroundings, a compilation of past experiences and make-believe notions. We've all done this to some degree—written out the script of our lives. We've brought our expectations into *this* relationship, into *this* situation, into *this* arrangement of circumstances. We haven't exactly been forthcoming with everybody about everything we've written, but that's mainly because we didn't really know we *had* these expectations until we were actually living in this present reality. Now that we're here—now that this is our experience—our expectations have come through loud and clear, stark and startling, bold and bright.

And it's going to take a real woman of grace to slip out of the director's chair and release her people from the fantasy world she's created.

Once we get really honest with ourselves, it's not so hard to see the damage our assumptions have caused. They are the flame smoldering underneath much of the conflict, tension, and dissent that resides in our home. So the woman resolved to live with grace, while not lowering her expectations, does intentionally recalibrate them. Rather than basing them on a fantasy delusion and forcing everyone else to fit in, she looks at her reality first and then, with the Spirit's leadership and counsel, shapes her expectations accordingly. She seeks to discern the true needs of her loved ones and then adapts her own view of things so that she can do what is best for them, nurturing an atmosphere in which they can genuinely flourish.

This is what grace does. It releases, frees, relaxes, unbridles. Allows room, loosens nerves, gives permission, expresses acceptance. One preacher described grace as an oil that lubricates friction and relieves tension. It is the WD-40 of life that eases rigidity and soothes the squeaky hinges. Grace is the smile that everyone you love is waiting to receive from you . . . so that they can finally be themselves around you.

It's time for this fantasy stage to fade to black. The lights and glamour just aren't ours to command anymore. Who wants them? We want authenticity more than scripted story lines. We desire genuine relationships and a relaxed atmosphere instead of all these painted faces and nervously protected conversations. We want life—*real life*—showered by a powerful, potent, palatable peace.

A woman resolved to grace can have exactly that.

• *Do you have a scripted play mapped out for yourself and the other people in your life? If so, how have you seen your loved ones negatively affected by your expectations? How has it negatively impacted you as well?*

• *Do you feel as though adjusting your expectations will amount to lowering them? Why?*

• *What other people, external pressures, or outside influences are contributing to the fantasy world you're attempting to force-fit onto your reality? How can you temper their effect on you?*

• *If you're the one being held hostage by someone else's demands and directives, how could you respectfully communicate your concerns and feelings and carefully navigate the situation so that you can experience freedom? And who can you enlist to help?*

Okay

*Sometimes when I just say, "Okay," the walls come tumbling down.
Those two little letters put an end to so many arguments. It's
amazing. Outside of calling on the name of Jesus Himself, I think
this is the next most powerful word in our language."*
—*A thirty-one year-old woman resolved to live with grace*

We like being right, and we want other people to agree that we are. That's why one of the hardest things to do in life, in marriage, in our homes and families, in our friendships, and certainly on social media is to resist the urge to flaunt that rightness. To win the argument. To send the other person away with his head hung in shame. We feel like our sentiments deserve the right to be heard, then understood, then agreed with and acted upon. And so we talk, and discuss, and post, and quit listening, and run the other person down. Into the ground. Into submission.

Those on the periphery steer clear, tiptoeing around the edges of the tension. They feel belittled and excluded. Out of favor. Blunted from expressing or even having an opinion.

All because everyone wants to be right.

But it won't be right. Not until someone is bold enough, confident enough, courageous enough—*gracious* enough—to kindly, lovingly, carefully acquiesce and say . . .

"Okay."

To finish it. Once and for all. Not because their demands were met, or their preferences catered to, or their position publicly affirmed, but because they prefer peace to madness. They desire restoration above discord. They want a home and a life that feels full, not depleted and empty—a hollow shell that echoes long and hard with the loud racket and chaos of a fiery argument, then turns cold and icy, bristling from the biting sting of silent treatments.

One little okay makes the difference.

This perspective is not modern. It's an ancient, scriptural sliver of venerated wisdom:

> *A gentle answer turns away anger, but a harsh*
> *word stirs up wrath. (Proverbs 15:1)*

Truly the wise woman doesn't always seek to be heard or validated but sometimes—in order to protect and preserve relationships, in order to invite peace back into her sphere of influence—she chooses a soft, delicate, gentle response in place of one that's sharp and explosive, harmful and wounding. She is resolved not to tend the fire of quarrelsome conversations, knowing she'll only be covered in its ashes long after the embers have burned out. She has a restraint that allows her to see through the veneer of out-of-control temperaments and off-kilter comments, down to the reality of the circumstance, recognizing that the thing she and the other person are making such a big fuss over is likely pretty small and insignificant in the grand scheme. She's not about to lose a precious relationship or to compromise her own peace of mind over a tiny skirmish on a miniscule hill. She doesn't stir the pot of people's emotions just for the satisfaction of watching them cave under the mounting pressure. She is patient. She brings calm to the storm.

And that's what makes her a picture of wisdom. And grace. A woman with the discernment of God's Spirit assisting her to weigh each situation as it arises. Because what she is *not* is a pushover. Not a doormat. She isn't being run over or made to cave to unhealthy, narcissistic tendencies. Neither is she cocky or arrogant with her okay dismissal. There's no air of sarcasm in her comment. No sinister smirk on her face. She's just strong. God has produced enough courage in her to prefer the long-lasting sweetness of deference over the small, fleeting, unsatisfying victory of winning this momentary battle.

So.

She.

Says . . .

"Okay."

Not easily but purposefully, powerfully, poignantly.

She inhales. Exhales. Forces a gentle sigh and a smile, coming up from somewhere deeper than human strength has the mining rights to dig. Then with a few simple letters, and one great big trust in God, she completely recalibrates this whole experience, not only for herself but for everyone involved—those she loves and is resolved to nurture.

"Okay," she whispers.

And in the end, she wins the greatest victory of all.

- *Prayerfully consider how you can apply the message of these verses in your life today:*

  - "A soothing tongue is a tree of life, but perversion in it crushes the spirit" (Proverbs 15:4 NASB).
  - "Patience can persuade a prince, and soft speech can break bones" (Proverbs 25:15 NLT).

- *Call a wise friend and discuss the difference between healthy deference and unhealthy silence.*

- *Making this resolution a habit in your most valuable relationships will take time and practice. Resolve to use this little word "okay" in this simple way, as much as you can in the next forty-eight hours. Record the impact it makes in your relationships.*

Grace

He was a struggling salesman, rising early each morning to go from one proverbial closed door to another, attempting to sell a variety of products made by the company he worked for. The days were long and exhausting, and he often had little to show for his efforts—certainly not from lack of trying, just from lack of takers.

His young, redheaded wife had been only eighteen when they married. And as their family grew, she spent the better part of each day trying to figure out how to make their small living quarters an enjoyable, satisfactory space, given the difficulties of their financial strain. Yet the day came when the strain turned into the kind that can make a girl want to give up—when she went to flip a light switch, and no lights came on. Thinking it was only a mishap in the electrical system, she went to another light source. Again, nothing. Another, nothing. Throughout the house she flipped switches—nothing—confirming what she already knew but didn't want to believe. Their electricity bill hadn't been paid.

Worse yet, it couldn't be.

So for the remainder of the day, she did the best she could to take care of her household responsibilities. Even as the lengthening shadows of late afternoon slowly shrouded the kitchen in dim light, she prepared a makeshift dinner, then set it out with care and dignity on their darkened dining room table. A flashlight search uncovered some half-used candles, which she lit to create an elaborate place setting. The scene was gorgeous.

When her husband arrived, tired and road weary, he found his family ready to have dinner with him. They enjoyed their candlelit meal. Had good conversation together. The children especially loved the unique touch of candles at dinner. Thought it was fun. Their home was full of peace and serenity despite the circumstances— circumstances the children didn't even know about.

Neither did her husband.

He went straight from the table and collapsed exhausted into bed, beside which she'd lit more candles. She never said a word. It wasn't until the next day, when he arose to get ready for work, that he realized there were no lights. Putting the mental pieces together, he realized what his wife had done—how she'd preserved his dignity, how she'd opted for peace and beauty rather than friction and discord in response to the inconvenience.

He walked past the bed one more time on his way out the door that morning, just long enough to brush the red wisps of hair from her cheek and whisper, "Thank you," into her ear. Whether she heard or not, he didn't know. But he was too grateful to let the opportunity pass him by. Grateful to be sharing a home—sharing a life—with a woman committed to being gracious, promoting peace, overlooking shortcomings, providing an environment in which her family could flourish, even when living in less than desirable circumstances.

In 1996, at their fiftieth wedding anniversary celebration, while adult children and grandchildren stood at their side, he recounted this story with the same endearing gaze set on his beloved wife. I was twenty-two years old then, and I've never forgotten it—this beautiful picture of a woman resolved to *live with grace*.

Whether you are married or single, your home is holy ground. Even if your home is just your room, whether in your parent's house or above the garage of another family, you are its holy attendant, bestowed with the responsibility and privilege of creating an atmosphere in which the essence of God's grace, freely extended to you, can be felt and sensed through the grace you freely extend to others. Your home is the place where you cultivate a peace to be enjoyed not only by the others who live there but by all who enter its doors.

Does that sound like a long shot to you? With all the chores to be accomplished, the stresses to be dealt with, the arguments to referee, the disorder to navigate? Maybe in your estimation your home is the *last* place where you think peace can ever really hang out.

And yet *you* are the person on whom it often hinges. We as women hold the primary controls to the mood, spirit, and quality of life within our homes. It's not about infusing more beautiful décor, more careful organization, better furniture, or updated appliances. (Many people have all these things and *still* no peace.) It's about recognizing your power to change the spiritual climate of your home based on your Holy Spirit-enabled resolve to be a woman who exudes a simple yet wonderfully poignant attribute . . .

Grace.

This was the advice I received from Rhoda, a pastor's wife ten years my senior, whom I'd known since I was a teenager. As we were just talking one day about our homes and families, she leaned over to me and said, "Priscilla, peace will be experienced in your home to the extent that grace is extended there. So dispense grace whenever you can."

Dispense grace.

Grace, by definition, is "favor or kindness expressed to the undeserving." It means giving someone a break when it's the last thing they deserve to get. And it is precisely what was given to us by God Himself when He extended to us salvation from our sins, despite the fact that we are dreadfully sinful.

> *For the law was given through Moses; grace and truth*
> *came through Jesus Christ. (John 1:17)*

Before Christ the Mosaic law was the standard by which God's people were to live—a list of rules and regulations that brought more guilt and shame every time they couldn't be followed. But when Christ came, He removed the people's fearful strain and bondage to a legalistic laundry list of demands, replacing it instead with the soft, wooing invitation to personal relationship with God (what He had wanted from His people all along). By meeting all the requirements of the law in Himself, Jesus ensured that our hope and salvation were no longer dependent on the way we tried to meet them. Instead of constantly working for His approval, we were just granted it. By simply believing in Him. Having faith in Him. Accepting His gift.

His grace.

And as a result, His freedom.

When we, as recipients of God's grace—His "gift" (Ephesians 2:8)—realize just how many bobbles and blunders of ours He lovingly forgives and forgets every single day of our lives, we suddenly find our motivation for extending that same undeserved favor to those around us. His patience, His acceptance, His understanding, His kindness. By His grace, they become ours—not just to *receive* but to *release*.

And when the people in your home and your life know that you won't look down on them or lord their inadequacies over them, you have given them a great gift. An overflow of the gift given to you. *Grace*. The gift of being able to stay authentic, knowing they'll be accepted just as they are.

Isn't that how you want to feel yourself? And isn't that the kind of freedom you want others to experience in their relationship with you?

Every problem, every issue, every potential disaster, every family member's weakness and failure, every less than desirable circumstance—when viewed through the lens of grace—becomes a fresh opportunity for extending mercy and kindness. Bestowing compassion. Seeing the best, even when the worst is front and center. Dispensers of grace are women who resolve to put candles on the table instead of sulking in the dark, women who don't want people walking on pins and needles around them, always having to accommodate their emotional mood swings or cover up their own failures for fear of being misunderstood.

Women who let peace reign.

Who let grace rule.

This woman resolves to make her home a safe place for her family and friends to find a haven from the world. Those who enter her doors find a serenity that grasps them, envelops them, soothes them, embraces them, drawing them in to dine around the table of peace and enjoy the company of those who are pleasurable to be around—because they're accepting, grateful, grace-filled.

It's revolutionary.

I mean, didn't grace utterly transform your life when Jesus gave it to you? If you were too young to know just how much of your life needed repair and repenting, hasn't His grace brought you to worshipful tears more times than you can count in the years since? Grace overwhelms. Everywhere it appears. Just think what it might accomplish when it comes gushing through your smile, your hug, your kiss, your tender pat on the back, your wink of forgiveness. Even *this* place, even *these* people could be completely renovated into something you barely recognize a month from now.

Like *you* were, when Jesus graced your life.

So take a little personal inventory.

- Are you easy to be around?
- Do you make it natural for your loved ones to feel accepted?
- Do you keep track of their mistakes and failures?
- When your family members do something with the intention of pleasing you, do they get to see a smile of gratitude brighten your face, or do you hardly even notice—won't give them the satisfaction?
- Do you hold others captive to your critical nature?
- Do you play the martyr because of all you're required to do?

Or . . .

Do you remember what Christ has done to cover every single, solitary failure of your life, freeing you from the bondage that would have kept you forever unsettled and unable to live abundantly? Do you eagerly express that same feeling of freedom to those in your home?

Give them a break.

I know they probably don't deserve it.

But neither did you.
Grace came anyway.

- *List three specific attitudes and actions that make grace palatable in someone's home life that you admire, not just in their interaction with you as company but with their family members as well.*

- *What do you feel will be the primary challenge for you in extending grace in your home? Be honest with God about this. Ask Him to "give you rest" and to let His "lowly and humble" heart be the one that comes shining through you (Matthew 11:28–29). It's Him. Not you. That's why they call it grace.*

Sabbath Spaces

On the morning of February 11, 2021, a winter storm warning was issued for all 254 counties in Texas, including where we live near Dallas. Subfreezing temperatures, mixed with all kinds of wintry precipitation, had already begun sweeping through the city, causing hazardous driving conditions and business closures. Clearly we Texans, who aren't exactly accustomed to cold weather and heavy snowfall, needed to brace ourselves for what was coming.

So we did.

And it was terrible, one of the most impactful winter weather events in state history. The eventual cost of the crisis has been calculated at more than a billion dollars, not to mention the ultimate cost of many lives lost. Power outages left millions of homes without electricity and exposed personal and corporate property owners to severe loss and damage. Grocery stores opened for only a few hours each day. But with nearly bare shelves, they could do little to provide help to those who braved the roads to get there.

At our house, where we holed up for the next four bitterly cold days, at times without heat, we wrapped ourselves in blankets layered over our thickest coats and camped out near the fireplace in the living room for warmth. We maneuvered through darkness with flashlights and spent hours playing rounds of board games by candlelight. That is, until the third day, when we heard a loud, mysterious gush of water coming from somewhere in the house. Our pipes had burst, causing water to stream down like Niagara through the ceiling and onto the hardwood floors. It meant cleanup and further disruption and—because of countless others going through similar situations—long wait times for repair companies and insurance adjusters struggling to keep up with the strained, widespread demand.

The troubles that everyone was dealing with ran from minor to major, the whole gamut. But among those who were spared the most tragic consequences, the thing you heard most on the news or from passing conversation was how strongly people felt about the one common facet of all our experiences: *staying home.*

Bear in mind, this storm occurred following a year when we'd already experienced unprecedented levels of lockdown due to the COVID crisis. We were much more accustomed than usual to dealing with this hunkered-down dynamic. Yet even with the 2020 experiences as pretext, people complained about a claustrophobia of cabin fever and boredom they couldn't wait to escape. Being at home with "nothing to do," forced to stay inside with their children and families, felt too restrictive. They wanted out. But some people (me, for example) rather enjoyed having all their brood together. Even now I look back on that aspect of the storm with a certain fondness and I've pondered these diverse reactions for quite some time.

- Why was being made to stay at home so hard for so many of us?
- Why was the idea of being untethered from our electronics so uncomfortable?
- Why were we so annoyed by having to come up with ways of spending time that were slow and easy?
- What's happened to the simple pleasures of home life that has taken away much of their endearment and attraction?
- Why couldn't we view this mandatory pause as a somewhat welcome interruption to our otherwise overcrowded schedules?

And yet according to the click bait of an online headline, people felt "stricken" by being stuck inside. Anxious to get back to the busyness.

That really says something, doesn't it? Are we so addicted to constant movement (addicted even to our stress!) that we just don't know how to relax anymore? Are we so driven toward performance and perfection that we can't see any value in a slowly paced day? Have we grown so accustomed to having no peace that we truly can't appreciate the beauty of it, even when given not only the opportunity to experience it but no other viable alternative? Worse yet, what are we showing the next generation—that there's nothing at all attractive about stillness, simple fun, and family time?

The woman resolved to live with grace rebels against our culture's resistance to rest. She understands that peace can only be experienced in her home if she purposefully creates margins to help herself and her family at least *occasionally* part ways from the hectic, demanding cycle of their usual activities. So she takes responsibility for planning deliberate opportunities for the age-old disciplines of rest and quiet. She is convinced that to "be still, and know that I am God" (Psalm 46:10 KJV) remains the most likely way for her and those she loves to sense His presence in her home.

I believe this principle is precisely what was on God's mind when He gave detailed instructions for Moses to relay to His beloved children of Israel. After nearly four hundred years of constant, grueling, daily servitude to Pharaoh in Egypt, this chosen generation had finally tasted freedom. And in the shower of God's deliverance, they were given (among others) this notable instruction . . .

"Remember the Sabbath day, to keep it holy." (Exodus 20:8)

"Sabbath" is from the Hebrew word *Shabbat*, meaning "stopping" or "cessation." God was requiring His people to do something exactly opposite from what they'd grown used to doing. Instead of endlessly working, one day after another, engaging in every demanded activity, they were to *stop*—to purposefully carve out time to be still and enjoy

Him—to celebrate a time of rest, rejuvenation, and spiritual focus that would perpetuate their experience of freedom, not just in theory but in the most practical terms. In other words, the Sabbath principle was the total reverse of the realities that slavery in Egypt had enforced on them. It provided protection against sliding into bondage of another form.

And while we are no longer subject to the Old Testament law, this principle of Sabbath still carries fresh impact for us. It should still shape our perspective and the way we approach our lives.

Our inclination toward incessant activity shows up in all of our crowded spaces—packed calendars, stuffed closets, jumbled minds that can't be turned off and quieted. We become slaves to busyness, slaves to the schedule, slaves to excess, which shows itself in disordered homes and disordered lives. We can't keep a single thought in our heads for more than thirty seconds. The roar never stops. We rarely just leave room for . . . *nothing*. Like Israel, we've grown so accustomed to constant activity that even when we can legitimately be still or preserve an empty space on our calendar, we feel unsettled. We feel guilty. We feel compelled to fill in every nook and cranny.

So in order to protect ourselves from being controlled and enslaved by our chaos, we must become women who intentionally create "Sabbath spaces"—margins in our lives that are left purposefully clean and clear so we can enjoy the liberty we've been granted by God Himself. Failure to do so will continue to result in more and more bondage.

Nothing is worse or sadder than a freed person slipping the chains back on—whether literally, figuratively, or spiritually. And unless we are deliberate about teaching this discipline to the next generation, we will be shackling them to the same chains of clutter that clank around our ankles most of the time.

But a new appreciation and gratitude for this Sabbath habit and lifestyle can begin with you.

I'll admit this pursuit is an ongoing challenge for me. With teenage sons who are growing up in a technologically driven age, the gift of boredom is often lost on them. Without my intentional (often exasperated) attempts at carving out tiny moments for putting our phones aside—like at dinnertime, for example—we might never have an opportunity to engage one another face to face. In actually real conversation.

One friend of mine finds this particularly difficult. While her family has decided to create a Sabbath space on Sunday afternoons to rest and be together, she often finds herself rushing around her living space trying to clean up, both implying and sometimes specifically demanding that her husband and children do the same. In the end no one rests or enjoys one another because mom is frantically prompting everyone to use their "rest time" to work! Letting her family just be and enjoy life is a real challenge for her. A discipline. It'll be a discipline for most of us too.

But let's do it.

Start with something I call the "14 Challenge."

Historically the Sabbath is one day out of every seven. This amounts to 14 percent of a week. So let's just keep it simple by starting with the number *fourteen*. Look at your schedule and decide where you could block out a Sabbath space of fourteen minutes each day— for yourself, for you and your husband (if you're married), or for your whole family to be together. Doesn't sound like much, but you might be shocked at how difficult this may be for you to achieve and maintain. You may also be amazed at how much this block of time could rejuvenate you.

On the weekends, encourage your children to spend at least fourteen minutes each day having some down time where they just go to their rooms to read or play quietly. This teaches both toddlers and teenagers that it's okay not to be constantly barraged by constant input—cellular data, video games, and other forms of entertainment that someone else provides for them. Your teenager might feel lost without TikTok or Instagram, but they'll get over it. And you'll be teaching them a valuable lesson.

As a married couple, Jerry and I have constantly had to work toward including this in the rhythm of our relationship. Wise mentors have encouraged us to find a weekend or full week that we can devote as a couple to Sabbath space, to rejuvenate and recalibrate from the other fifty-one weeks of the year. Even after two decades, we are still working to prioritize this. It easily succumbs to other, seemingly more urgent family demands. But when we do include it in the cadence of our lives together, we find it strengthens our relationship and increases our intimacy. Find a way to incorporate rest into your marriage. You need this and so does your husband. So does your relationship.

This doesn't necessarily mean taking a costly vacation *to* a particular destination. Sometimes it only means taking a vacation *from* certain activities. A simple week "off" from inundating technology and the normal schedule can give you a refreshing boost, as well as the opportunity to do some things you don't usually have time for—like, for example, visiting an elderly relative, reading a novel cover-to-cover, cleaning out your closet, organizing last year's photo memories, or just taking an extra nap or two. Prioritizing a Sabbath will cause you to be fresher, lighter, and more prepared to take care of your home without becoming so easily frustrated and stressed out.

But beyond just planning breaks in your time, consider creating Sabbath spaces in the tangible areas of your home. As easy as it is for our calendars to become overrun with responsibilities, our own homes can also turn into pits of clutter and chaos, causing them to feel less like a haven and more like a cave or dungeon we want to get out of. So why not create some "margins" in your home as well? Just as you cleared fourteen minutes from your daily schedule, clear fourteen inches of space somewhere in your living area once a week.

Maybe that untidy shelf of yours is forty-eight inches long. Discipline yourself to clear just over one foot of space. Then the following week, fourteen inches more in another area of your home. Don't go overboard trying to do a major house cleaning and organizational sweep or get overwhelmed because you can't do everything at once. As an act of obedience to God—even an act of praise-filled worship—start giving your home some breathing room. Deliberately own that small section of your world until you've transformed it from piles of junk into peace and joy. Do it consistently enough, and you'll wake up one day a few months from now with a living space that's orderly, balanced, and more available for God's use, all in fourteen-inch increments at a time.

I know there's nothing much more refreshing to me than walking into my closet and . . . *actually being able to walk in*! I enjoy being able to choose an outfit to wear when I can actually slide my clothes across the bar and see clearly what I'm choosing from. If it's so crushed and crammed that I can't even move the hangers from side to side, I get frustrated and put out. But what if it was fourteen inches more livable this week, and then I made another area of my home fourteen inches more livable the next? Pretty soon, I'd be 100 percent satisfied.

So think about it. Is there a shelf you could clear out in your hall closet this week—just one small area where you could reclaim some space in your life? Is there a nook or corner that's become a dumping ground for stuff that could be sifted through and given to someone who really needs it? Is there a single countertop that could be swiped clean of unnecessary untidiness that's serving no real purpose? What about the junk drawer in your kitchen that holds everything and nothing at the same time? What will be the line, the "stopping point" for all your stuff?

Only the woman living with grace and pursuing a peace in her life will exercise the necessary restraint and discipline to prioritize Sabbath spaces. Sure, it will be an ongoing and constant challenge. You may only be able to inch toward it, not leap into it at one big swoop. It may happen in varying degrees during different seasons of life, and it will definitely require the Holy Spirit's empowerment to maintain. But give yourself grace and keep growing. Instead of feeling uncomfortable with silent, empty areas and unfilled spaces, guard and embrace margin. See it as the gift from God it is meant to be in your life.

Remember, nothing is enjoyable when there's too much to be enjoyed. You'll never be able to fully utilize what's at your disposal when all the important things are lost under a pile of miscellaneous things. So take a few minutes to look carefully at your time and space, then determine that the claiming of peace is more important than hanging on to all this stuff that is slowly, methodically claiming you. Let go and usher in an environment of peace into your home so that it becomes a place to be enjoyed, not burdened by, not enslaved to.

A Sabbath space.

You need it in your home, in your day, in your week, in your life. If you don't have any idea how to put it there, grace can do it for you.

- *As you move forward with signing this resolution, carefully consider the practical aspects from each of these chapters that will need to be layered into your decision. What are some things you can begin to put in place to make grace and peace realized in your home?*

❧ LIVING WITH GRACE ❧

I will cultivate a peaceful and grace-filled life where everyone can sense God's presence not only through acts of love and service but also through the pleasant and grateful attitude with which I perform them.

———————————————

LEAVING A GODLY LEGACY

A resolution to live today with tomorrow in mind

Choose Wisely

A good [woman] leaves an inheritance.
(Proverbs 13:22)

My brother once met an interesting young man while visiting a church in another city. After becoming acquainted and spending some time in casual conversation with each other, he began to tell my brother about his family which, it turns out, bears quite an interesting legacy.

His great-great (however many "greats" make seven generations' distance) great-great grandfather was a prominent political and military leader in the newly formed United States of America. He presided over the Constitutional Convention in May 1787 and wielded significant influence over the structure and ratification of our innovative form of government.

In fact, he became our first president.

But during those formative years in our nation's history, with many decisions to be made about how this republic should be organized and function, a relatively small yet vocal group of citizens had interest in making George Washington king instead of president, eager for his leadership skills to be put to more permanent use. This would mean that subsequent men in his family would automatically ascend to the throne and carry the title. And he likely had the power to make it stick if he'd wanted to, especially if he'd thought it would be in the best interests of the nation.

"In other words," this young, direct descendant of George Washington said to my brother, "I could be king right now if he had chosen differently."

One decision.

Made by one person.

Shaping and impacting reality for seven generations and beyond.

I wonder if George Washington had this reality in mind as he was making his decision. I'm curious to know if any thoughts concerning his legacy were at least part of his rationale when choosing what he would do and what he wouldn't. I can't ask him, of course, but . . .

I can ask *you*.

Are you making today's decisions with their impact on tomorrow in mind? When you're arranging your priorities and forming your habits, do you think about your children, your grandchildren, about the kind of character they'll remember about you and inherit from you? When you spend your money, or sport your fashion sense, or post your comments, or spare your time, does it ever occur to you that you're not just making a choice for yourself, in the moment? That you're making a choice which impacts people who are following behind you? That you're perhaps playing a role in the attitudes and observations of a young woman you hardly know, maybe even a total stranger who one day hears someone telling what you were like?

These are the kinds of questions to keep in mind when thinking about what you will do today. How you will respond in this moment. The kind of restraint you will exhibit. What type of resolutions you will make and live by. These decisions matter right now, and . . .

They *keep* on mattering.

They are your legacy.

They are your inheritance.

When my paternal grandfather passed away in December 2019, we found he had left to us—his grandchildren—a financial inheritance. We were grateful, but also shocked. We had no idea this quiet, humble, unpretentious man who'd lived in the same row house in urban Baltimore for more than six decades had been steadily saving up for us.

This is the kind of "inheritance" most people think of when they hear that word. A gift bequeathed to others after a person's death. An estate. Usually the terms of this transfer are carefully spelled out in an organized, legal document, detailing exactly how gifts of land, money, property, and possessions are to be distributed to a person's loved ones. Clear instructions about who gets a certain piece of jewelry or a particular item of furniture. Yet as valid and honorable as it is to make these kinds of arrangements, cementing the tangible connection between generations, people tend to spend more time planning their physical inheritance than their spiritual one.

So, again, while I'm grateful for a grandfather who wanted to bless us with his material savings, I'm eternally more grateful that he had been just as methodical and intentional about leaving other things behind for us that money can't buy.

Our legacy of faith as a family was carefully crafted and passed on by him as he made daily decisions to live with integrity, instill responsibility, endure through hardship, and model honorable living. Virtues like these—compassion, gratitude, perseverance, forgiveness, patience, and love must be stewarded and then purposefully passed on in order to survive from one generation to the next. Things that aren't earned by shrewd investing but by simply living. Gifts that aren't reserved for major holidays and dressy events but are given out on Tuesdays and Saturday mornings, in your sweatpants, without a lot of fanfare and fireworks.

Just you. Choosing to live today as if someone's tomorrow depends on it.

This seemed to be paramount in Moses's mind as he stood on the outskirts of the land of promise, having sojourned with God's people forty years in the wilderness. Here he was, 120 years old, nearing the end of his life, sharing the crucial messages on his heart in these final hours with his beloved friends and fellow citizens (Deuteronomy 28–30).

. He spoke of legacy.

He spoke of spiritual inheritance.

He encouraged God's people to make today's decisions with tomorrow in mind.

See, I have set before you today life and prosperity, and death and adversity; in that I command you today to love the LORD your God, to walk in His ways and to keep His commandments and His statutes and His judgments, that you may live and multiply, and that the LORD your God may bless you in the land where you are entering to possess it.... So choose life in order that you may live, you and your descendants. (Deuteronomy 30:15–16, 19 NASB)

By choosing to love the Lord, to cling to Him, and commit themselves to Him in faithful obedience—*today*—the people of God could expect a long, prosperous existence as a nation *tomorrow*, filled with a lifetime supply of His joy and peace. This would allow them and their children to be recipients of all the benefits stipulated by the covenant God had initiated with them. In return for their faithful choices, they would be assured of "life"—a promising legacy of divine protection and provision to be handed down to their children and grandchildren as a heritage and birthright.

I wonder if the men and women hearing Moses' words, thinking about what God was offering—I wonder if they looked down at their children, milling and playing around their feet, picturing them all grown up and experiencing the full, rich benefits of their parents' obedience—a mom and dad who chose to live in a way pleasing to the Lord.

I wonder, too, if they were equally lost in thought and in visions of the future when Moses presented the second alternative: *death*. Making this selection would result in consequences that were equally explicit—things like misery, loss of divine favor, the insecurity of living outside God's protection. Terrible stuff. Horrible, long-lasting side effects. Worse than the kind they rattle off on those prescription drug commercials that come on while you're cooking dinner.

Two choices. Life. Death.

Was there really a choice to make? Would anyone knowingly seek "refuge in his own destruction" (Psalm 52:7 ESV), squandering the opportunity to bequeath a steady, godly legacy to his children, complete with all the blessings and favor that comes from God alone, both for themselves and the generations to come?

Yes, they would.

And yes, we do.

Both knowingly and unknowingly, we do it every time we make even small, daily decisions that are contrary to the purposes, plans, and promises of God. We sign our names to a rotting, moth-eaten inheritance that those whom the Lord has entrusted to us will one day receive. When we ignore God's priorities and make unwise, self-centered decisions without concern for others, we take a hammer to the legacy we'll leave behind. We bequeath instead a heritage of heartache, turmoil, adversity, unnecessary difficulty, and possibly even spiritual curses to contend with.

Perhaps you know this reality with startling clarity. Maybe you are a product of the unwise choices of your parents. The legacy left to you has been one of addiction and compromise, of debt and unforgiveness, of failure and shredded self-esteem. Maybe your parents didn't mean to leave you imprinted with this kind of heritage, and yet they did—every time they chose not to specifically, purposefully, consistently make their momentary decisions with tomorrow in mind. When they opted for pleasure and fun over purity and fidelity, when they opted for weakness and selfishness over willful obedience and steadfast love, they were making the unwitting decision to pile baggage on your grown-up doorstep, the kind of clutter that can often take years to clear away.

But no matter what legacy has been handed down to you, you can wake up in the morning to draft a new one on the drawing board of your life. You can restructure the clauses. Refocus the points and paragraphs. You can rename the recipients and reorganize the types of gifts you intend to give. This is your opportunity. To leave a legacy. A different legacy. A new legacy.

And it all starts today.

With the decisions you'll make right now.

This was Eileen's reason for living well. She was a mother with eight children. Her husband worked consistently and diligently to provide for the family, traveling incessantly and doing his best. But it was no easier on Eileen, who lost two of her children to death at birth, struggled with her own health, and was even forced at one time to make a transglobal move with her family to keep hope afloat. Life was hard. Every day harder than the one before. But she had decided as a young woman that she would cultivate a legacy worth leaving to those she loved. So despite the many difficulties and challenges, she made each day of her life a decision to pay her legacy forward. To stay committed to her family and faithful to the Lord. To sit all eight of her children around her knees to read Scripture and pray over them. To invest herself fully in the work God had for her. It was difficult, but it was worth it.

Before she went to heaven at the ripe age of ninety-two, she had the joy of sharing her life with thirteen grands and twenty-one greats to go with her already enormous brood. You could see the sparkle in her eye when surrounded by the fruits of her labor. She watched her posterity soaking in the favor of God's protection and provision, and took the deep breath of a woman satisfied. You can still see the framework of God's blessing in the lives of those who trace their history to her door. You can see that her wise decisions paid off.

This, too, can be your legacy.

And, no, it's not too late.

Today—truly, within the next twenty-four hours—an eye-opening choice is set before you. It's disguised as your next opportunity, your next option, your next decision, your next offer. Now's your chance to see these through the lens of Moses' biblical description. See them as small yet significant choices between death and life.

Is there really a choice to make?

Choose life.

Choose wisely.

The legacy you are leaving depends on it.

- *How have you seen (or perhaps tasted for yourself) the long-lasting fruit of personal choices on the lives of others? How have you been harmed by them? How have you been blessed by them?*

- *What are some of the choices you already know about—ones that are coming up in the next few days, weeks, or months— that will provide you the opportunity to make an impact on your legacy? What can you do now, ahead of time, to ensure that you choose wisely?*

- *List the people most important to you that you desire to leave a godly legacy to.*

Unexpected Legacy

She sat across from me, steaming coffee cup in hand, leaning in to our conversation—the same way she always does every time I talk with her—intent, personal, intimate.

My aunt, all seventy-five years of her, was sharing the morning's rainy moments with me in my home, nestled on my well-worn sofa, engaging in some girl talk during her yearly visit to the States from London. In her unmistakably British accent, she shared with me what the Lord had been teaching her lately.

I listened.

I mean, I *always* listen to her.

I've never found her insights to be anything less than thoroughly captivating and thought provoking. A deep student of the Bible, her understanding of spiritual things wafts through the air like the familiar floral aroma of her favorite perfume. She's never lacked for stories about the happenings in her life. Her frequent travels to countries I've never even heard of have made for fascinating tales. In sharing God's Word with different people groups around the world, she's seen miracles and moves of His Spirit that can make your eyes pop out of your head. The detail with which she describes His marvelous work, things she's seen up close and personal . . .

Breathtaking.

But at this moment she was even more intense than usual, peering from behind her brown, square-rimmed glasses, her hands grasped tightly around her warm coffee mug, just as her sentiments began to clasp around my heart. Because on this morning, she spoke of personal things.

Of singleness.

Of childlessness.

Her journey has been filled with longings and losses in both areas. She's never been married. She was on the cusp a couple of times, but . . . never ultimately felt God leading her to covenant her life with either man. And she's okay with that. Over time she's made peace with it, with what's appeared to be God's calling on her life to remain purely satisfied in Him. Took time, yes. But it happened.

And yet . . . childlessness . . . perhaps something even deeper in a woman's psyche than the desire to find her heart's true love. That's why years ago when she went to the doctor complaining of certain pains and discomforts in her body, his recommendation that she undergo a hysterectomy struck her at a depth of sorrow she didn't realize she was capable of feeling. To permanently close off from her the opportunity to reproduce life erupted in the form of deep, raw, lonely emotions that are no less staggering for a single woman than one married. It's the ripping away of a desire that dwells at the core of womanhood—doesn't matter what her status is. Were God ever to choose a husband for her, she now knew with certainty she could never bear children.

Coming to grips with singleness had been hard, she told me. Coming to grips with childlessness had unexpectedly been harder.

By the time of her surgery, however, she had let God deal with much of her pain and loss. In fact, one day while recovering in the hospital, she heard a baby crying in the near distance. And amazingly, instead of the sweet sound rushing over her with another wave of heartache and grief, it compelled her to seize the moment as an opportunity to receive her season of barrenness and to walk within it wholeheartedly—to surrender instead of fight against what the Lord was allowing. As she did this, a consuming sense of freedom surged through her body. God placed a blanket of His peace and contentment around her in a remarkable way. She knew that He was bringing her through this ordeal victoriously. She felt like He was saying to her, "You have given up the physical womb, but I have given you a spiritual womb."

Nearly six months later, while attending a meeting at church, she and a small gathering of brothers and sisters were in the pastor's office, praying passionately and earnestly for God's work and God's people. During the course of their praying, a wise, godly mentor—who actually knew nothing about her experience of release and surrender those many months earlier—slipped over to where she was, placed a loving hand across her shoulder blades, and said to her in words that supernaturally confirmed God's leading, "You are not barren. Out of your womb will come new life. There is life to be produced and a legacy to be left through you. You have daughters, many of them."

Many of them.

Perhaps you know my Aunt Ruth's heartache. Perhaps you feel cheated from experiencing a biological legacy. But maybe, if you look carefully, you'll see the same thing God opened my sweet aunt's eyes to see—spiritual offspring, a plethora of daughters, just waiting to be imprinted with wisdom and counsel and encouragement and favor . . . with the embrace of someone's motherly love.

As women in whom God's Spirit lives and has borne fruit, we have each been called to leave a godly legacy, to pass the baton of His grace and truth to others who will then take it to lengths and destinations we will never go ourselves. This is not an option. This is a heavenly mandate.

How unjust it would be for God's work in your life to start and stop with you. Your lifespan is simply not long or large enough to contain the heights and depths of His activity, then to swallow it whole without offering anyone else a bite.

This heritage must be carried on. And it can be.

Through you. To them.

This truly is the essence of what a godly legacy is—the continued sharing of values, standards, beliefs, disciplines, priorities, experiences, lessons learned—not only to those who sprout from your family tree but also to those with whom you share the bloodline of Christ.

- *If this chapter speaks of your story, what does God seem to be specifically saying to you through it?*

- *Who are some younger women that come to your mind who could benefit from a mentoring relationship with you?*

- *If perhaps this chapter doesn't apply to you personally, how could you use its truths to both encourage and challenge the single, childless women in your life—to invest themselves in the responsibility of legacy building?*

Set in Stones

"What do these stones mean to you?" (Joshua 4:6)

In any other place, they might be just rocks. Gray, bland, boring, stagnant pieces of creation, good for little other than holding down the end of your picnic blanket or cracking open a nutshell.

But put those rocks on the banks of the Jordan River, marking the site where two million Hebrews closed the book on forty years of wilderness wandering, walking across on dry ground into the promised land—a milk-and-honey moment they'd been waiting their whole lives to see—and suddenly these are not just rocks anymore. They're monuments.

And that's exactly what God intended when He said to Joshua . . .

"Take for yourselves twelve men from the people, one man
from each tribe, and command them, saying, 'Take up for
yourselves twelve stones from here out of the middle of the
Jordan, from the place where the priests' feet are standing
firm, and carry them over with you and lay them down
in the lodging place where you will lodge tonight.'"

*So Joshua called the twelve men whom he had appointed from the
sons of Israel, one man from each tribe; and Joshua said to them,
"Cross again to the ark of the LORD your God into the middle
of the Jordan, and each of you take up a stone on his shoulder,
according to the number of the tribes of the sons of Israel.*

*"Let this be a sign among you, so that when your children ask later,
saying, 'What do these stones mean to you?' then you shall say
to them, 'Because the waters of the Jordan were cut off before the
ark of the covenant of the LORD; when it crossed the Jordan, the
waters of the Jordan were cut off.' So these stones shall become
a memorial to the sons of Israel forever." (Joshua 4:2–7 NASB)*

Rocks. Just rocks. Until they are gathered, strategically memorialized, and purposefully positioned to be remembered.

Most of us would probably categorize our days as an array of mundane, normal experiences. It's what we do. It's who we are. It's how we get from point A to point bedtime. From good-morning to good-night. But take a woman resolved to leave a godly legacy, and she begins to realize that these moments stand for more than mere calendar dates and common occurrences. They are the ongoing testaments of God's work in her life. They represent experiences with Him that are unique and personal, as noteworthy and significant as they are normal and second nature.

They may just be Mondays, but they are still monuments.

So I'm asking you today to become intentional about gathering up these "stones," about building a record of what God is doing in your life. Instead of spending every other night this week on something that will probably yield little if anything of real value, would you be willing to take just one slice of one evening to walk back into the middle of the Jordan—into some moment when you experienced God in a memorable way—and pull out some insights that could help begin construction on a growing record of your legacy?

Your legacy. It needs a script for others to follow. Both you and they need a way to remember.

Now let me preface what I'm about to share with you by confessing that I'm not all that fantastic when it comes to journaling. I wrote a little something in my journal last week, and it was my first entry since, oh, nine months ago? How's that for consistency? I've always admired those women who keep a beautifully bound, leather journal in the top drawer of their nightstand, pulling it out every evening like clockwork, recording in flowing prose their experiences of the day. I'd love to be like that. Maybe one day I will.

But even though I've not been terribly dependable in this department, I'm grateful that it has remained an overarching habit through the years. I'm the type of woman who journals when . . .

- something is pressing on my heart and mind.
- a specific milestone has been reached.
- the Lord has been doing an important, transformative work in me.
- I'm in the middle of a particular life occurrence that seems to hold implications I just know will matter in the future.

Fairly average days and events, in most respects. And yet the only thing that really makes them forgettable is when I fail to record them.

So how happy I am that I've done this through the years. Even the most sporadic sentiments have been impactful to look back on. To be able to recall specific seasons of life, to remember exactly what I was praying for, then to recognize more clearly than ever how the Lord responded—few things are more faith building and encouraging to me. It's like pulling down a photo album and flipping through the pages, reliving scenes you're so glad you captured when you had the chance. Some are from big moments—family vacations, birthdays, Christmas Eve. But others are just from offhand afternoons when you saw something you wanted to keep and treasure. Recording God's handiwork, in ways both large and small, provides you and others a walk down memory lane that inspires because it's a reflection of Him walking with you.

And now, because it's recorded, it's set in stone.

The day will certainly come when those to whom you desire to leave a vibrant spiritual heritage will be interested in seeing how you handled even an ordinary moment from an ordinary morning, how God's faithfulness and care and protection and guidance intersected your path one day and turned it into much more than just a routine traffic stop. Your children, your grandchildren, the younger women you hope your life will be able to affect—they'll be curious to see how He moved and worked, through both your successes and your failures, your high spots and your biggest mistakes, wrapping them all in His sovereign grace and (with your cooperation) sealing them in ink on these simple pages.

It's good reading. Legacy making.

I've found this to be so valuable and rewarding, in fact, that I've started a journal for each of my sons. On occasion when I see the Lord moving in their lives, or I notice them reaching a new level of maturity in a particular area, I open up their little book and make a record of the experience. Even if I only think to do it once a year on their birthdays, my goal is to give it to them later when they're old enough to appreciate a mom's look back at their spiritual growth and development, insights that their wives and children—wow, my grandchildren—will find intriguing and priceless, even hilarious in spots. But a legacy all the same. Continually rolling forward. Connecting generations. God be glorified.

If you've tuned me out here because you just have no interest in writing things down—again, I understand. My siblings and I have a father who is that way. One Christmas we went to great lengths to find a perfect journal for him, one with a genuine leather cover. Lush and masculine. Quite pricey even, but we thought it was worth purchasing for him. We hoped it would span the generations. We had his name engraved on it and presented it to him with great pomp and circumstance, believing he'd enjoy having it on his desk and writing little nuggets to us whenever he had something special to pass along to his children for posterity. That way we'd always have a record of these important sentiments of his.

That was a decade ago. The journal is still on his desk.

And it is also still empty.

My point is—I'm not really asking you to resolve to journal—to do it in this one way and this one way only. I know the pen-and-paper method just doesn't match up for everybody. I get that. But I *am* asking you to find your own way to store up your legacy. To gather stones.

Obviously the life you are actually living in real time is much more important than the one you write down. The way you respond in practical, consistent ways to Christ's lordship is of much greater real-world importance than how a journal remembers it. But as a woman of resolutions, you bear a responsibility to others. This is not just about whether you like to do something. It's about priority. Purpose. Promises.

So . . .

- talk into a voice recorder
- create and save short video clips
- download or order an annual scrapbook
- record your devotional thoughts in short snippets in the margin of your Bible or in the notes section of your online Bible app
- type up a prayer and save it as a Word document

Maybe just searching back as far as you can on your social media feed will give you a perfect place to start. But save those sentiments. Capture your thoughts and the happenings that went with them.

Find your own unique way to do it, but don't leave your children and grandchildren without something to see and touch and feel and hear—something that shows what God has done to bring you and them to this moment in time. It's a masterpiece in the making.

Every day your Father does something new. He molds and shapes. He guides and refines. He rotates and contours and buffs around the edges. Every single day. And though it may seem all routine and ordinary to you, this is the stuff of your legacy. It's happening all around you. Inside you. In living relationship with the One you long for others to know in ever deeper ways, to ever greater extents. And one day, way sooner than you think, when they come to you wanting to know, "What do these stones mean?" . . . make sure you have something to show them, not just tell them.

You are a woman whose story bears reading and repeating because your God is doing amazing things in you, whether or not you realize it. Things you don't want to hide and downplay. Things others shouldn't need to learn all over again. Things that will help them launch into life with a spiritual boost and a head start.

That's the strength of a woman's legacy. *Your* legacy.

Built on a Rock. Carved in stone.

- *This final section and its resolution are the climax of every other one we've made. The primary purpose of these resolutions has been to assist and support you in leaving a legacy you can be proud of. So right here, as we end our journey together and turn the final pages of this book, I ask you to use this last experience as the opportunity to prayerfully tie together everything we've been learning and committing to doing along the way.*

  These have not just been pledges to become a better person. This is about living a life that's bigger than yourself, one that can't be contained by the limits of a human lifetime. This is about both responsibility and joy—the responsibility to invest heavily in others and the joy of watching God take our smallest gifts and turn them into eternal treasures.

  In whatever way He leads you to do this, He will supply you incredible grace and strength to accomplish it as you walk through the different seasons and struggles of your life. Resist the urge to strive. Just resolve to point the compass of your choices in the direction of these resolutions, and then trust your loving Father with the outcome.

  As you make this final resolution, realize you're making a truly lasting difference, and that your commitment to and continued growth in these thirteen resolutions will make an impact for generations to come. Give yourself grace and keep going! You, a woman of great resolves, are establishing a godly legacy.

❧ LEAVING A GODLY LEGACY ❧

I will make today's decisions with tomorrow's impact in mind. I will consider my current choices in light of those who will come after me.

_____

THE RESOLUTION FOR WOMEN: AT A GLANCE

I WILL *embrace my current season of life and live with a spirit of gratitude and contentment.*

I WILL *champion God's model for womanhood and teach it to my children.*

I WILL *celebrate my God-given uniqueness and the distinctions He has placed in others.*

I WILL *live as a woman answerable to God and faithfully committed to His Word.*

I WILL *seek to devote the best of myself to the primary roles God has entrusted to me.*

I WILL *be quick to listen, slow to speak, and esteem others more highly than myself.*

I WILL *forgive those who have wronged me and reconcile with those I have wronged.*

I WILL *not tolerate evil influences in myself or my home but will embrace a life of purity.*

I WILL *pursue justice, love mercy, and extend compassion toward others.*

I WILL *be faithful to my husband and honor him in my conduct and in my conversation, and will aspire to be a suitable partner for him to help him reach his God-given potential.*

I WILL *teach my children to love God, respect authority, and live responsibly.*

I WILL *cultivate a peaceful and grace-filled life where God's presence is sensed.*

I WILL *make today's decisions with tomorrow's impact in mind and consider my current choices in light of future generations.*

I WILL *courageously work with the strength God provides to fulfill this resolution for the rest of my life and for His glory.*

As for me and my house, we will serve the Lord. (Joshua 24:15 NASB)

Notes

1. *"Hosanna,"* Words & Music by Brooke Fraser © 2006 Brooke Fraser/Hillsong Publishing (Admin. in the U.S. and Canada at EMICMGPUBLISHING.COM).

2. Gary A. Haugen, *Just Courage* (Downers Grove, IL: InterVarsity, 2008), 1.

3. Shaunti Feldhahn, *For Women Only* (Sisters, OR: Multnomah, 2004), 93.

About the Author

Priscilla Shirer's voice rings with raw power and clarity in packed-out arenas, conferences, and churches throughout the nation and the world, where for twenty years her passion to teach God's Word unapologetically has never wavered. Whether through her speaking ministry, her best-selling books and Bible studies, or even on a movie screen, her primary ambition is clear—to lift up Jesus and equip His children to live victoriously.

Priscilla has been married to Jerry Shirer for twenty-three years. Together they lead Going Beyond Ministries, which exists to serve believers across the spectrum of the Church. To date, the ministry has released more than a dozen video-driven studies for women and teens on a myriad of biblical characters (like Jonah, Elijah, and Gideon), as well as topical studies on *Discerning the Voice of God*, *The Armor of God*, and others. Priscilla has also written a fiction series called *The Prince Warriors*, in addition to award-winning books like *Fervent* (ECPA Christian Book of the Year) and her best-selling devotional, *Awaken*.

She and her family make their home near Dallas, Texas, where between writing and studying, Priscilla spends her days trying to clean up after (and satisfy the appetites of) the Shirer men, including her three rapidly growing young adult sons.

Other books *from* Priscilla Shirer

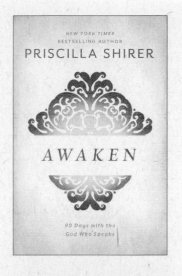

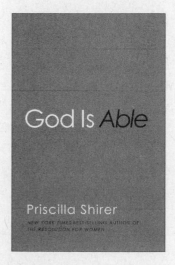

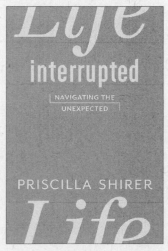

These and more available where books are sold.

Bible studies
from
Priscilla Shirer

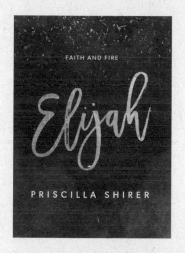

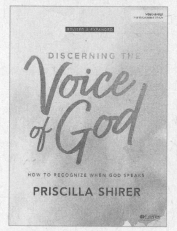

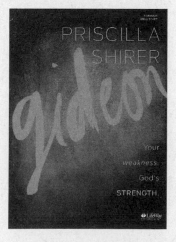

These and more available where books are sold.

Inspiring a Revolution

What does it look like when a man takes full responsibility
for himself, his wife, and his children?

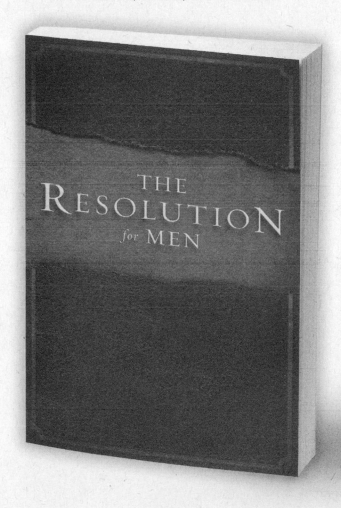